2001

University of St. Francis Library

W9-DGB-370

ENHANCING  SOCIAL STUDIES

 THROUGH

LITERACY

 STRATEGIES

by
Judith L. Irvin
John P. Lunstrum
Carol Lynch-Brown
Mary Friend Shepard

Florida State University
College of Education
Tallahassee, Florida 32306

LIBRARY
UNIVERSITY OF ST. FRANCIS
JOLIET, ILLINOIS

National Council for the Social Studies
Founded 1921

President
H. Michael Hartoonian
Hamline University
St. Paul, Minnesota

President-Elect
Pat Nickell
Fayette County Public Schools
Lexington, Kentucky

Vice President
Richard Diem
University of Texas
San Antonio, Texas

Board of Directors
Janet K. Adams
Peggy Altoff
Sara Smith Beattie
Adrian Davis
Tracy A. Dussia
James J. Elliott
Joseph Roland Gotchy
Sandra Haftel
Stephen Johnson

Terry Kuseske
James Leming
N. Nanette McGee
Thomas M. McGowan
Jeff Passe
Denny L. Schillings
John Solberg
Robert J. Stahl
Carole J. Wilkinson

Ex Officio
Mary Teague Mason
House of Delegates,
Steering Committee Chair

Executive Director
Martharose Laffey

Publications Director
Michael Simpson

Editorial staff on this publication: Lynn Page Whittaker, Salvatore J. Natoli, Pamela D. Hollar
Art Director: Gene Cowan
Cover: Paul Wolski

Library of Congress Catalog Card Number: 95-070506
ISBN 0-87986-067-7

Copyright ©1995 by National Council for the Social Studies
3501 Newark Street, NW • Washington, DC 20016-3167

All rights reserved. No part of this publication may be reproduced, stored in a retrieval system, or transmitted, in any form or by any means, electronic, mechanical, photocopying, recording, or otherwise, without the prior written permission of the copyright holder.

Printed in the United States of America
10 9 8 7 6 5 4 3 2 1

First Printing, August 1995

372.83
I712

■ Table of Contents

■ Preface

Enhancing Social Studies Through Literacy Strategies was written for social studies teachers who want to help students improve their literacy abilities while enhancing the teaching of social studies content. Research shows that how students learn in social studies and how they learn in literacy seem to follow parallel paths. That is, the more students engage with content and concepts, the more effectively they will learn.

Reading in the content areas has been a high priority concern of educators since the 1970s. This concern continues in the present decade, and has expanded to the other aspects of language: writing, speaking, and listening. In this volume, we present approaches and strategies for integrating literacy acquisition with social studies content and processes, for deepening student understanding of the social sciences, and for motivating students to read and write in the social studies class. Although based on current theory and research, this book is practical in nature. It is intended to be a handy reference tool for busy teachers in planning creative and challenging social studies classes.

Some of the special features of this volume are: 1) a review of current thinking in literacy education and student motivation; 2) step-by-step procedures for teaching social studies vocabulary while emphasizing concept development; 3) literacy-based strategies to develop critical thinking abilities; and 4) guidelines for fostering reading of historical-content trade books by students and a recommended list of historical literature appropriate for teachers to read aloud to students or for students to read independently.

As teachers seek to meet the ever-increasing demands of classroom interaction, we hope this book will provide useful strategies for improving the literacy ability of students while enhancing the teaching of social studies.

Chapter 1

Enhancing Literacy Abilities Through Social Studies Content

Social studies is the integration of history, the social sciences, and the humanities to promote civic competence. It can also be defined as the study of social relationships and the functioning of society, including the study of interactions among people and groups of people. Historical events, political issues, economic policies, and archaeological discoveries are caused by people. Learning about those people brings the social aspect to the study of social studies.

Learning language is a social event, too. We speak, listen, read, and write to communicate with other people. Enhancing the literacy abilities of students enables them to participate more fully in society by interacting more easily and willingly with others and by being able to communicate in more ways. Communication is essential for harmonious social relationships and for the efficient functioning of society.

People interpret what they read in light of their experiences. For example, if students relate their own feelings of perceived parental repression to the causes of the American Revolution, they may better understand the motivation of our country's founders; if students visualize the living conditions of primitive cultures, and relate those conditions to their own culture, they may understand how the decisions of earlier Americans have affected their way of life. Because social experience informs and helps us to interpret much of what we read, it seems natural to use social studies content to help students improve their ability to read and write. Literacy, defined as reading, writing, speaking, and listening, can be taught, reinforced, and strengthened through learn-

ing strategies to help students understand social studies concepts.

The focus of students' early years in school is on learning to read and write. Students also need to understand the importance of "reading and writing to learn." Students continue learning to read and write while improving their literacy ability through the content they are studying. The authors of *Becoming a Nation of Readers* make this point quite strongly: "[T]he most logical place for instruction in most reading and thinking strategies is in social studies and science rather than in separate lessons about reading" (Anderson, Hiebert, Scott, and Wilkinson 1985, 73).

This chapter presents an overview of literacy instruction in the social studies. It begins with an outline of the evolution of views on content area reading and writing and presents an overview of current thinking on the process of learning. We discuss some of the challenges facing social studies teachers and present a case study. Suggestions for motivating students to read and write in social studies conclude this chapter.

Evolution of Views on Content Area Literacy Instruction

The idea of integrating reading and writing instruction with subject matter instruction is not new. Moore, Readence, and Rickelman (1983) showed that work has been done in this area since the early 1900s. It was, however, the publication of Harold Herber's *Teaching Reading in the Content Areas* (1970) that focused educators' attention on the need to integrate content areas and reading instruction.

The evolution of this concept can be summarized in three words: skills, guidance, and strategies.

Skills

The notion that every teacher is a teacher of reading met with justified resistance two decades ago. At that time, the emphasis was almost solely on reading and not writing. The prevailing means of teaching middle and secondary school reading during that time was skill-building. That is, reading skills were taught in isolation, on the assumption that they would, at some future point, be applied to the act of reading. For social studies teachers, this type of instruction would have meant setting aside teaching content to use phonics workbooks, skill sheets, and controlled readers instead. Teachers were not trained to teach reading, nor did they want to spend time teaching reading. Social studies teachers simply did not feel comfortable with the idea of teaching reading. One course at the preservice level or a few inservice sessions could not prepare a teacher trained for secondary social studies to teach reading in this manner.

Reading specialists hired to work in secondary schools diagnosed and worked with students individually outside of the classroom. Most reading specialists taught reading as a series of isolated skills, and instruction was often brought down to the students' reading level. The trouble with this approach is that students still had to return to their social studies class and attempt to read their assigned textbook.

Guidance

This phase in the history of content area literacy instruction was intended to help students learn content from their textbooks. Again, the emphasis remained on reading, to the exclusion of other aspects of literacy.

Guidance is typified by the study guide: students were guided through reading. The guidance orientation was an improvement over the skills orientation in that students were improving their reading abilities in conjunction with learning content from their textbooks. Although some of the study guide activities included previewing and summarizing activities, little instruction was included on how to read and understand a textbook. The reading portion of these exercises was somewhat rigidly defined: finding the main idea, putting events in sequential order, and locating information.

Social studies teachers resisted writing, using, and correcting study guides because it was time-consuming. They seemed to prefer other methods of teaching the history, government, and geography they were trained to teach. Many teachers avoided the textbook and used simulations, debates, movies, and other non-print media to teach the facts, concepts, and generalizations of social studies content.

Strategies

This phase in the history of content area reading focuses on learning strategies in all areas of literacy: "Researchers have identified certain mental processing techniques–learning strategies–that can be taught by teachers and used by students to improve the quality of school learning" (Derry 1989, 4). Strategies, then, are processes that help students become thoughtful and deliberate in their approach to a specific learning task such as reading or writing. A student who can efficiently solve the problems demanded by such a task is said to be "strategic."

Helping students become strategic learners is not unlike the inquiry methods most social studies educators learned in methods courses in college. Learning strategies and the inquiry method contain prereading activities that serve to activate and connect what a student already knows about a topic to the new information under study. This prior knowledge is then used as the investigation continues and is refined as new and former knowledge is synthesized. Because this stage of synthesis often draws on writing or results in written compositions, social studies teachers are naturally inclined to use the content of their subject—history, geography, social or political science, economics, and anthropology—to teach students to read and write strategically. In fact, many social studies teachers, through the inquiry method, have been facilitating reading comprehension and developing writing abilities in students for years. What has been missing, however, is the knowledge of reading and writing processes so that teachers could help students understand and monitor their own cognitive processes.

Teaching social studies content through the inquiry method and teaching students to be strategic readers and writers are compatible endeavors. Students must read, write, and think about something. Reading and writing abilities can be developed using almost any kind of content. Thus, helping students become strategic readers and writers is in harmony with good teaching of social studies content. Strategies, in fact, should be taught in the context of academic content. The key to this integrated instruction is the teacher's knowledge of how students learn language. With this knowledge, a teacher can use content to develop proficient, thoughtful, and strategic readers and writers. This development in language ability will in turn enhance the learning of content. Because of this reciprocal relationship, teachers have much to gain by teaching reading and writing using social studies content.

The Process of Learning

The basic premise of learning is that new knowledge must be connected to existing knowledge, whether at the level of a single concept or when working with a larger, more complex set of ideas. Proficient learners build on and activate their background knowledge before reading, writing, speaking, or listening; poor learners begin without thinking. Proficient learners know their purpose for learning, give it their complete attention, and keep a constant check on their understanding; poor learners do not know or even consider whether or not they understand. Proficient learners also decide whether they have achieved their goal, and summarize and evaluate their thinking. Social studies teachers can instruct students in the learning behaviors that proficient learners use; an example follows.

Suppose a social studies teacher wants to teach a unit on consumer economics. She assumes that her students understand few of the economic concepts, but she needs a starting point. The first question she must ask is "What do my students already know that can be related to the information I want them to know?" She knows that her students are familiar with buying and selling. As consumers, they have well-developed knowledge about many products and types of commonplace business transactions.

The teacher capitalizes on this knowledge. She sets up activities that bring out students' knowledge of the marketplace, discussing everything from video games to the price of a school lunch. Then, she relates these experiences to the topic of consumer economics, thus building upon old concepts in order to develop new ones.

This teacher has activated and built upon her students' "schema" of consumer economics. "Schemata" comprise all of the information and all of the experience that the reader has stored in memory. A particular "schema," then, represents all of the associations that come to mind when a person reads about a certain subject. By activating a schema closely related to the subject of study, a teacher can provide students with a framework in which new facts and concepts can fit. In this case, all that students know, have experienced, and feel about their own economic consumption can help them understand new concepts in economics.

Thelen (1986) likened schema to a file folder. Everyone has a unique and personal way of organizing cognitive structures (the cabinet). The schemata are the ideas (folders) contained within the cabinet. Learners must figure out where and how new material fits into the existing structures. Because each learner has his or her own organization, it is important that teachers help students engage their own schema; then, the students can connect new information to what they already know.

Of particular concern to social studies teachers are the problems of inaccurate or fallacious schemata in the minds of students (Camperell and Knight 1990). Science teachers have also had to face this problem in explaining the physical world to their students. The task is far more difficult and complex for social studies teachers who must deal with problems of prejudice and stereotypes deeply embedded in existing schemata of students. Unfortunately, a rational refutation of such views usually encounters strong resistance. Teachers can use learning strategies to encourage students to examine ideas that challenge their own beliefs. The tasks of helping students become aware of their existing schema and then cultivating a climate of open-mindedness to facilitate the restructuring of those schema is the process that improves the understanding of social studies content.

Students reading a textbook know they are understanding new information when it fits into their existing schemata. Proficient and active readers check periodically to make sure they are understanding what they read. Poor and passive readers read along whether they are comprehending the material or not. When having problems comprehending a passage, proficient readers call upon a bank of strategies to correct the misunderstanding. They may choose to read on, go back, or ask someone but they do something to help them understand the text. A similar process occurs with writers: good writers monitor their writing for accuracy and comprehension, whereas poor writers write down words and ideas without considering whether they make sense. The process of monitoring reading and writing progress and selecting strategies to deal with specific problems is called metacognition.

Metacognition generally has two components: knowledge about cognition and regulation of cognition (Baker 1991). These two components of metacognition involve the ability to reflect on one's own thinking and include knowing about when, how, and why to read and write. This ability includes understanding ourselves as learners and what the task demands. Suppose, for example, a student is approaching the task of reading a chapter on South Asia. She looks at the pictures in the text and concludes she really does not know much about this area of the world, except for flooding in Bangladesh, an assassination in India, and wars in Afghanistan and Vietnam. She decides to rely heavily on the maps, charts, pictures, and text to understand the content. Previewing the chapter, she also recognizes that she will have to depend on the context to understand the meaning of certain words. This student may also decide that, to understand the relationship of ideas in the text and to study for the short essay test, a chapter map would be helpful in organizing the information. While she is reading and completing her chapter map, she evaluates her comprehension of the text.

Metacognition develops as students mature, usually during adolescence, but teachers can teach and strengthen it by explicit instruction and practice (Palincsar and Brown 1983). When teachers understand the process of learning and become proficient in strategies that enhance learning, students naturally benefit. Teachers who understand the learning process can help students: 1) activate their prior knowledge; 2) monitor their comprehension and composition; 3) apply strategies as needed; and 4) organize and store information for later retrieval. Teaching students to become strategic readers and writers enhances the teaching of content; students who can read strategically understand better what they read, and learn content more efficiently.

Motivating Students to Read and Write in Social Studies

A common theme runs through the concerns voiced by social studies teachers at all levels: that is, how to combat students' apathy and disinterest and build their motivation to learn. Inherent in teaching literacy in the social studies are some continuing problems, or perhaps challenges, that teachers must face. These challenges involve textbook difficulty and limited reading ability of some students.

Dealing with Text Difficulty

Many teachers use the textbook as their sole or major resource for social studies instruction. This practice creates the problem of trying to make the textbook intelligible and interesting for the students. Sadly, few if any social studies textbooks compel a reader to pick them up to read during one's spare time. Consequently, students have difficulties reading and interpreting most social studies textbooks (Estes and Vaughn 1985).

In an analysis of middle school American history textbooks, Armbruster and Anderson (1985) found complex organization and questions to be the pattern. They concluded their study by saying:

> We are struck by the complex world of middle grades social studies text structures, question types, the background knowledge required, and the sheer amount of information that students and teachers face. . . . each of these factors comes to bear on the complicated task of teaching students to read in the content areas. (65)

At the intermediate elementary grade level, teachers expect students to become independent of the teacher in reading assignments. The predominantly narrative materials usually found in basal readers are replaced by more expository materials usually found in social studies textbooks. With the exception of the literature-based readings in English classes, secondary school students continue the trend established in intermediate elementary school to read expository text materials. Attaining independence in reading the basal reader in elementary grades does not necessarily prepare students to read their social studies texts independently (Herber and Nelson-Herber 1987).

Students must learn to adapt their reading ability to a variety of reading materials. Ideally, students should receive a gradual introduction to reading expository texts in the elementary schools. As Herber and Nelson-Herber (1987) note, "At each grade level, in each subject area, teachers must help students learn to read to learn at a level of sophistication consistent with the concepts and resources being studied" (586). Becoming an independent learner is a lifelong process, but all too often systematic instruction in reading ends in grade five, and that instruction may be limited mostly to narrative material. Learning strategies may help students become strategic readers and writers so that they can read difficult texts more successfully.

Coping with Limited Reading Ability

A second factor affecting reading problems in social studies is the limited reading ability of some students. Recent national studies have documented that students at various ages read better in 1984 than students at the same ages in 1971. However, 40 percent of 13-year-old students and 16 percent of 17-year-old students attending high school still have not acquired intermediate reading skills. Thus, many of these students are unable to search for specific information, interrelate ideas, or make generalizations about the social studies content. The inability to perform these tasks raises questions as to how well these students can read the range of academic material they are likely to encounter in school (*Reading Report Card* 1985).

Many of our nation's youths have significant reading disabilities and find social studies textbooks difficult to read because we have paid little attention to helping students become strategic readers. Teachers, however, must strengthen student motivation if they are to help students improve their reading in social studies.

The Case of Tim Enfield. Tim Enfield is a classic example of the unmotivated student. Every teacher will be able to relate, at least in part, to Tim's attitude toward reading and his behavior in the classroom. Tim's case illustrates the need to identify and use student interests, build background information, and activate prior knowledge to motivate students to read.

Tim, age sixteen, had somehow managed to get to the tenth grade, although all indications from test data suggested that he had a reading level of about grade two. He was generally considered a discipline problem and viewed by some teachers as hopeless. When he appeared in his social studies class, he asked to be moved away from other students. Still, his teacher felt that Tim had some potential and set about the task of finding out more about him. She described him as follows:

Tim's interest in reading is limited both in school and out. In fact, he expresses an aversion to books. His reading at home seems to be confined to the *TV Guide* and magazines dealing with firearms. He is interested in hunting and fishing. He also has some interest in drawing, primarily cartoons. He has mentioned using topographical maps. Subjects liked least in school included English, math, and science. He has a motorcycle he rides after school. Preferences in music are exclusively country and western.

In the excerpt that follows, the teacher begins an interview to learn more about Tim by raising questions about his interest in guns and his perceptions of reading:

Teacher: One of the things I wanted to ask you is how you managed to obtain all this information about guns. You probably

didn't get it through a lot of reading.

Tim: No.

Teacher: Did you talk to a lot of people about it?

Tim: Yeah, I talked to a lot of people and jes herded it up.

Teacher: What are some guns that you have in your collection?

Tim: I got Brownings, Remington, Mossburgs, Winchesters, Colts, and a Kentucky muzzle loader pistol, and uh, a little Russian-made derringer, both with black powder.

Teacher: You told me earlier you were interested in the uses of black powder and you were talking about the Kentucky rifle. You mentioned that in addition to the Kentucky rifle there was another rifle used on the frontier. . . .

Tim: Yeah, the Hawkins.

Teacher: The Hawkins? O.K. And what was the difference between the musket and these frontier rifles?

Tim: Well, the Hawkins had a heavy barrel on it. Really, what that was good for was the mountain men . . . always kept getting knocked off their horses by trees 'n stuff and the stocks kept breaking off or they'd break a barrel or somethin'. And they had to have a gun heavy enough and sturdy enough to go out and knock down some of this North American big game like grizzly and moose 'n stuff. And the little forty-five caliber Kentucky flintlock wasn't heavy enough. And it was too long to maneuv– . . navigate through brush and undergrowth, so they had to have a gun heavy enough and short enough to get the job done.

Teacher: Very interesting. Let's come back to your reading for a minute. What do you do when you come to a word you don't know?

Tim: Try to figger it out, but mostly ask somebody.

Teacher: Tim, what do you think reading is?

Tim: Huh, well, I guess jes readin' words.

The preceding interview contained several surprises for Tim's teacher. First, Tim's oral vocabulary was more extensive than his reading vocabulary. His use of the words "navigate," "derringer," "undergrowth," and so on underscored a verbal facility not previously observed in class. Another surprising factor was the depth of his knowledge about firearms, acquired through his listening ability.

Tim's oral reading of social studies materials (even at fifth-grade reading level) was characterized by numerous miscues. Tim read reluctantly, under much tension, showed anger and frustration and, on some occasions, with a few whispered four-letter words.

Tim's teacher wondered how well he would read when he encountered a selection within his interest area. She gave him something to read written on the 11–12th grade level but definitely within his interest and background experience: firearms and hunting. Tim read an excerpt from a manual on firearms; he had not reviewed it previously.

Tim's reading, while not fluent, indicated an understanding of what he had read, pronouncing words such as "flintlock" and "percussion capped muzzle loader." At one point, he even stopped and explained a term to the teacher. A discussion of Tim's reading level seems irrelevant since his ability to read depends on what he is reading. The important role of background information and experience was made clear to Tim's teacher.

Tim's Perception of the Reading Process. Far too many poor readers such as Tim have seemingly learned to view reading as simply a word recognition, or word calling, process. Later in the interview, other questions shed light on Tim's language processing ability. When asked about his reading, Tim said despondently, "I got to more or less struggle. Most of my teachers think I'm dumb." He traced his problems in reading back to second grade when, in Tim's words, "The teacher kept drillin' on all those

rules about what sounds those letters make." It seems that Tim had a different model of reading than his second grade teacher.

Tim's social studies teacher decided to use a language experience activity in a modified form to see if it would help Tim gain some insight into the events surrounding the onset of the American Revolution. Recalling his interest in guns and drawing, she drew Tim's attention to the famous portrayal of the Boston Massacre when, on that fateful day in March of 1770, British troops had leveled their muskets and fired at a group of demonstrating citizens. Paul Revere's famous engraving of this event (which was used as propaganda to mobilize sentiment against the British) is featured in most U.S. history texts but is often passed over with little comment.

As Tim studied the picture, he listened to a brief taped explanation of what was happening in the scene. Next, he listened to another tape of an excerpt from a contemporary British textbook describing the scene as primarily unwarranted mob action directed against the hapless British soldiers. This was, of course, at variance with the traditional American patriotic version. Tim was then asked: supposing you were a British cartoonist of that period, how would you have shown this scene? Tim discussed with his teacher what possible differences might be shown between the American version from the pen of Paul Revere and what a British artist would show. Then Tim, armed with pencils, pens, and drawing paper, went to work.

After working in the library for two periods and on his own at home, Tim produced a cartoon that clearly showed the Boston colonists demonstrating in aggressive postures, threatening a hapless, terrified British sentry who had no recourse but to summon help. Tim was then asked to dictate on audiotape in his own unrehearsed words, what he was saying in his "British version" of the Boston Massacre. Reproduced below is Tim's explanation of his sketch of the Boston Massacre:

This is what happened in the Boston Massacre. This poor soldier was standing up on there guarding the plank so no unauthorized persons could get on board their boat and there was a whole pack of bullies that come there and started making fun of him and kicking dirt on his shoes and getting his uniform all dirty. So the soldier ran for to get some help and these eight soldiers came up there with their guns and bayonets fixed more or less to frighten them away. But the bullies went and got help too. They got knives, pitchforks, snowballs and stood there throwing things at those guys. One of the Americans got a gun and fired. And the poor old British soldiers thought somebody got killed on their side and they shot into the mess too.

To his surprise and pleasure, Tim was able to read aloud his story of the Boston Massacre a week later with no help from his teacher, who was equally surprised and pleased by his correct use of such words as "unauthorized." One can see how Tim brought his own background experiences to bear in the interpretation by use of the idea of "bullies" preying on the frightened men. With some help, Tim edited his story and presented the cartoon and interpretation to the class. His presentation startled but impressed his classmates who had previously viewed Tim as an oddity and an outsider. The praise and recognition he received led Tim to undertake other cartoons depicting colorful personalities in U.S. history and significant events. This process made it necessary for Tim to seek out books, read to the best of his ability, and ask questions.

Using Varied Materials to Motivate Students

Like Tim, all students must relate to a topic personally to generate and maintain any interest in learning about it. In fact, to learn anything, one must connect new information to what one already knows. Activating and using schema about a topic are imperative

before new learning can occur. It, therefore, seems logical to connect the new learnings to what students know about how people relate to each other.

For social studies classes, a rich array of materials is available to stimulate interest and deepen understanding of selected issues or themes. In chapter 4, we will discuss the use of narrative literature in teaching social studies. Some examples of other material stressed here include domestic and foreign newspapers, documents, plays, photographs, drawings, posters, postcards, maps, and social studies materials designed for students in other countries.

Newspapers. Newspapers are clearly a popular medium of mass information that has long held appeal for conscientious social studies teachers seeking ways to bring the realities of world affairs into the classroom. The movement to provide practical and pedagogically sound applications of newspapers to the classroom continues to gain strength. More opportunities are available today for social studies teachers to apply this popular medium. The movement, under the umbrella of the Newspapers in Education (NIE) program, reaches an expanding audience. There are some 600 individual programs in the United States, Canada, and Australia which support the use of newspapers in various fields and at both the elementary and secondary levels (Kossack 1987). Professional organizations such as the International Reading Association have joined newspaper publishers to provide support and professional credibility to a movement that reaches varied audiences with its diverse materials including feature articles, editorial pages, classified advertisements, and letters to the editor.

A good example of what teachers can do to relate newspaper reading to social studies themes is found in the *Indianapolis Star*'s publication, *A Salute to the Constitution and the Bill of Rights* (Yeaton and Braeckel 1986). In this book designed for teachers grades 4–6, practical and interesting activities use newspaper articles to show how the Constitution and Bill of Rights work. The activities draw on a broad spectrum of newspaper features. One exercise shows how to relate a comic strip such as "Nancy" or "Dennis the Menace" to a constitutional issue. Another approach confronts students with an Associated Press dispatch headlined "Students Can Be Suspended for Vulgar, Offensive Language." A reading of the article with the aid of the teacher provides a springboard for examining the issue of freedom of speech.

Shapley (1986) offered specific suggestions on how to reinforce law-related education in social studies by using the newspaper. Some of these suggestions include:

1) Ask students to find articles explaining the treatment of citizens in other countries by their legal systems. Then, have them compare and contrast how the same individuals would be treated in the United States legal system.

2) Follow a jury trial in a local paper. Role play the trial as the action unfolds and predict the verdict.

3) Assign students to read and discuss articles relating to environmental laws. Have them draw up a cause-and-effect chart and trace the environmental issues over a period of weeks. Encourage students to make predictions about court decisions which affect the environment.

Teachers can stimulate student interest in the editorial pages and letters to the editor by exposing students to conflicting views about significant public issues at relevant points in the course. The next step is to encourage students to examine the basis for differing views on the same issue and then to identify assumptions made by the various writers.

Newspapers also provide an avenue for initiating a study of advertising as an economic and social force. Students can learn much about this fascinating industry and trigger interest in reading about its origins, growth, contributions, and shortcomings. From a comparative study of advertising in different time periods, students can also learn much about changing cultural ideals or standards as suggested in the following activity. A middle grade social studies teacher had her students compare selected examples of advertisements in the late 1800s derived from a book illustrating Victorian advertisements (DeVries 1968) with contemporary newspaper advertisements. The students were asked to analyze both sets of advertising using a checklist based on Maslow's hierarchy of basic needs (Maslow 1970). The students were amused and intrigued by the persistence of certain types of advertising that appealed to concerns of maintaining or regaining health and well being.

Visual Materials. Increasing professional interest in visual literacy–interpreting pictures and drawings–has emerged in the last decade. Sandler (1980) has presented a model for analyzing pictures in a textbook through a questioning procedure, culminating in the collection and classification of data and the formulation of generalizations. Allen and Felton (1986, 21) proposed using historical photographs to "excite students about their history" and as a means of "getting them to use information to learn how to think." The photographs to be chosen should include both cultural and physical elements of human life. In addition, it is important for the photographs to reflect a certain ambiguity about what is depicted in order to arouse curiosity and facilitate the questioning process.

In a questioning model, students are encouraged to speculate about what is depicted in the illustration, to draw inferences, and test those inferences. In one example, Allen and Felton use an old photograph of sugarcane syrup-making in the nineteenth century. The authors have published study prints from several periods with background information and a guide for using the questioning model that teachers could apply easily to studying a variety of historical illustrations. Teachers could adapt the Allen and Felton approach where museums and public libraries have rich resources in historical illustrations.

An even more promising approach in using visual materials stresses the use of "mysteries" in geography and history (Allen and Felton 1986). A mystery is an important but puzzling situation containing discrepant data and difficult to explain. The use of mysteries appears to be consistent with what is presently known in the psychology of learning about interest-promoting techniques. "Presenting students with factual information which contradicts their present knowledge and beliefs," observed Mathison (1989, 171), "creates what educational psychologists refer to as a dynamic disequilibrium." For a number of years developmental learning theorists have attested to the persistence of a strong human drive to regain a cognitive equilibrium (Erikson 1950; Harvey, Hunt, and Schroder 1961). Hence, a motivational drive is triggered as students read further in an effort to restore their "cognitive equilibrium" by finding a rational explanation for the given mystery.

Teachers may use the literature of tourism–travel posters, advertisements, and even postcards–to build interest in reading about various countries and peoples. Allen (1989) proposed an activity for world geography employing travel posters. Teachers can use these posters in such a way as to "disrupt student expectations," a research-verified, interest-promoting technique (Mathison 1989, 171). When we disrupt the learning expectations of students, Mathison noted that we counter boredom and lack of interest and "induce a temporary state of surprise and confusion that heightens student interest in textbook information."

In one teaching episode involving a class of seventh grade world geography students about to undertake a study of sub-Saharan Africa, students entered their classroom one day to find taped to the walls vivid tourist posters of Botswana, a nation in the southern region of Africa. Displayed on the posters were colorful scenes of the Kalahari desert and various wild game. Postcards were passed around the class as students studied the posters and viewed a world map showing the location of Botswana. Following Allen's model lesson, students were first asked if they would like to visit this place. The teacher then probed their responses to reveal reasons and reasoning.

In the second phase of the lesson, students were asked to write a brief paragraph about what they thought life would be like for the people who lived there. They shared their accounts, reading aloud their impressions, which largely portrayed Botswana as a rather primitive society where people worked mainly on game reserves, engaged in marginal farming activities, and lived in round mudhuts. In the third phase, students then turned their attention again to the posters, postcards, and samples of tourist advertisements (e.g., photographic safaris and bird watching in the Okavango Delta, and treks into the Kalahari). The fourth phase found the teacher raising questions about how certain words from the posters or tourist literature were used to create images of this developing African society.

At this point, the teacher challenged the students to test their images of this nation by drawing on reliable current information about Botswana. Students could obtain some information from the text and more up-to-date and detailed information in the media center–particularly nonfiction and reference works including almanacs and encyclopedias. In addition, the teacher could plan in advance for this lesson and secure copies of *Background Notes on Botswana* (1990) from the U.S. Department of State. (The State Department publishes in the form of these notes highly readable, reliable profiles of life and culture in most countries of the world.) Maps and summaries of economic, historical, and political data are also included. For this teaching activity, the teacher had obtained copies of newspapers from Botswana published in both English, the official language, and Setswana, the national language. The teacher instructed students to find articles that reflected life styles, interaction between people and their government, and economic and social concerns. To their surprise, students found that Botswana was a multiracial democracy with a stable multiparty parliamentary government and a proven record of sound economic development.

As the students examined the newspapers and other reference materials, they found evidence of growing cities and towns and modern urban life styles as well as a vital traditional culture evidenced in kgotla (council) meetings, in customs, beliefs, and values of villages. They also found indications of the social problems that accompany rapid economic growth. Students were compelled to restructure their view that led them to conclude initially from the tourist materials that Botswana was simply a primitive, turbulent part of Africa—an impression all too often stemming from uncritical television viewing or superficial treatment of this complex, vast continent in school texts and other media (Crofts 1986). The lesson stimulated much interest in further reading about Africa and Botswana. Allen's article includes other motivational follow-up activities such as constructing a more accurate poster of Botswana and writing to tourist agencies and embassies to caution against the superficial images often contained in the literature of tourism. Included with the lesson plans applicable to countries in Asia, Africa, and Latin America are sources of information that will enable teachers to secure the materials needed from embassies and travel agencies.

Social Studies Realia and Field Trips. Objects, documents, artifacts, and field trips can bring a deep understanding and appreciation for the lives, values, and formative historical experiences of the peoples and cultures treated in the textbook. A number of social studies educators including Jarolimek (1990) have underscored the importance of realia and field trips in developing interest in learning social studies content. Field trips to museums, national historic sites, archaeological digs, law-making institutions, and courts can bring a sense of reality to topics and issues presented in social studies. They may also serve as springboards for further investigation and reading. Careful planning and preparation of students is, of course, essential. In the following paragraphs a broad spectrum of realia are suggested as useful sources of information.

Documents are perhaps one of the most readily available and adaptable resources at the disposal of the social studies teacher in both elementary and secondary levels. By "documents," we refer to historically and politically significant objects including maps, records, photographs and drawings, letters, and posters. The National Council for the Social Studies through its official journal, *Social Education,* maintains a regular department called "Teaching with Documents." Education specialists from the Education Branch of the National Archives and Records Administration serve as editors for each feature in which a document is reproduced and featured. The specialists also provide lesson plans for class use of the documents, which may be reproduced for classroom presentation through the use of transparencies or slides. In many instances, teachers may utilize Allen and Felton's model for analysis of visual materials or create their own mysteries to be resolved.

Some of the varied and stimulating documents from *Social Education* and other sources include the following:

1) A photograph of a land auction in California at the beginning of the twentieth century suitable for use as a mystery (Alexander 1979).

2) A map particularly suitable for a discovery-type mystery exercise is an actual archaeological site map drawn by anthropologist Richard Lee of a Bushmen encampment in the Kalahari desert in Southern Africa. A preferred and less ethnocentric designation today of these people is the San people. Originally the map was designed for the Anthropology Curriculum Study Project in the late 1960s and was first published by Macmillan (*Studying Societies: Patterns in Human History* 1971). This map is now available in the form of an activity to teach economic concepts in world studies from Joint Council of Economic Education (O'Neill 1980).

3) Census records of 1880 in the Dakota Territory and in 1900 in Missouri showing where some favorite figures of children's literature, Laura Ingalls and Almanzo Wilder, lived. Students may have assumed these were not real people, and teachers may arouse their interest in encouraging them to read further about life on the frontier in this period. The census rolls are reproduced showing the names of the Ingalls and Wilder families and information about them recorded at that time. Teachers are advised (Mueller and Schamel 1989) how to secure historical census data for their counties if they wish to encourage their students to reconstruct a segment of their own local history as reflected in the lives of the families listed in the census records.

4) A poster advertising "Americanization Schools" in Granite City, Illinois. These schools were set up in the period following World War I to help in the assimilation of large numbers of immigrants arriving in this period (Alexander 1979). Such posters may be used to encourage reading and reflection on what life was like for many immigrants in America. The teacher may then introduce the concept of the new wave of immigration from Hispanic and Asian countries and encourage students to read accounts of what their lives were like before coming to America.

5) Baseball cards may seem an unlikely stimulus to reading, but Vernon (1988) showed how a baseball card from the National Archives reveals much about changing values in American society. The lesson plan contains suggestions on how to develop insights into one aspect of social history and raises questions concerning the opportunities and limitations of major sports as a vehicle for upward mobility. The card selected for study is that of a colorful player of the 1950s, Minnie Minosa. Even before Jackie Robinson integrated the major leagues, Minosa was one of the first of the black Latin American players to gain wide recognition among U.S. baseball fans. The baseball cards of the period were fairly durable with eye-catching appeal and interesting facts about players.

Baseball cards from the Archives can be used to study the transition occurring in the industry in the 1950s. Students may be interested in further reading about baseball and baseball cards. Some books that middle school and high school students might enjoy include Jules Tygiel's *Baseball's Great Experiment: Jackie Robinson and His Legacy* (1983) and Stephen Clark's *The Complete Book of Baseball Cards* (1982).

6) Letters from people addressing vital issues and concerns can also bring a sense of reality to the classroom and focus attention on books dealing with the issues. The files and archives of local and state historical societies may contain many letters. You can usually secure copies of such letters and use them in class to arouse students' interest in a period, showing how real men, women, and children reacted to the conditions of life and the major events of the period.

To encourage inquiry into conditions of life during the Civil War, one might draw on the letters of soldiers and members of their families on both sides of the conflict. Davis (1974) illustrates the values of letters in an inquiry lesson incorporating the letters of the son of one Georgia family during the Civil War.

In a class in sociology, a teacher might focus attention on the adolescent subculture with letters (Mueller 1985) written to President Eisenhower from the ardent fans of Elvis Presley pleading that their rock and roll hero not be drafted into the Army in 1958. Since there is no record as to how President Eisenhower responded to this plea, students may construct what they believe—given the circumstances—is an appropriate response.

In a more serious vein, a documentary approach to the study of the civil rights movement could draw on letters from private citizens seeking to draw the attention of their government to the persistence of segregation, notwithstanding the 1954 Supreme Court decision. One 1961 letter (Alexander, Byers, and Freivogel 1978) from Mrs. Osceola Dawson to the Interstate Commerce Commission eloquently expresses her indignation at efforts in southern states to retain segregated facilities for railroad travelers.

Using Controversial Issues to Build Motivation

This country has had a strong educational tradition of supporting the use of controversy in the classroom. John Dewey (1933) claimed that learning increased as insight arose from a problematic situation. In the 1950s and 1960s, two influential social studies theoreticians, Hunt and Metcalf (1968), argued persuasively that the most productive learning emerges from situations in which "the most cherished beliefs of students are felt to be at stake" (293). They challenged social studies teachers to emphasize in their courses what they termed

"closed areas"—specific areas of beliefs and behavior that they identified as largely closed to rational thought. The history of academic freedom and censorship in this country includes a sufficient number of incidents to explain the reluctance of some social studies teachers to present anything that smacked of controversy. Today, the situation has improved since the constraints on freedom of teaching that operated in the early years of the Cold War. The strong support of teacher organizations on behalf of the freedom of teaching and the freedom to learn, advancements in teacher education, and recent decisions supporting the pedagogically sound use of controversy by both federal and state courts have contributed to a climate more conducive to the treatment of controversial issues.

Expanding on this rationale, we offer a model for a planned use of the study of controversial issues to encourage further reading by students. The literature of the social studies has proposed other models for treating controversy at one time or another. Certainly models such as the jurisprudential approach of Oliver and Shaver merit careful consideration. Many of these models, however, require extensive inservice education and much teacher preparation. We propose a five-step model that teachers can adapt readily to most students in social studies without extensive teacher reorientation. Our major focus at this point is not to develop a highly sophisticated model for decision-making but rather to encourage students to recognize the value conflict that characterizes most significant controversies, to refrain from the rush to judgment, and to undertake further reading and study of the issue.

The five steps involved in this model (Lunstrum 1981) are summarized below:

Step 1. The teacher would explain that, as part of the overall objectives of the course, the class from time to time will examine areas of controversy, and students will be encouraged to consider conflicting views and examine their own beliefs. The teacher may wish to point out that the right to privacy and other rights of students will be respected. The role of the teacher in the expression of opinions may be reviewed and explained. In some communities, it may be necessary to pursue this in greater detail, citing local school policies supportive of the need in a democracy to prepare citizens to examine controversy and discipline it along intellectual or ethical lines. (If no local policy is available, one from a national education organization, e.g., NEA or NCSS, may be used.) It will not be necessary to repeat the orientation step on every occasion when controversy is studied. However, when the issue is likely to trigger a marked increase in the level of dissonance, it will be helpful to remind students that the purpose is not to exacerbate conflict but to help students acquire the knowledge and skills essential to effective participation in a free society.

Step 2. Create an awareness of a significant controversy. Significant decisions or events in history and court cases in the study of government are potential springboards for indepth study. Textbooks often tend to avoid controversies and may treat a significant conflict in public policy superficially. Pervasive conflicts between national security and personal liberty often escape scrutiny in the tendency to cover the text. An example may be found in the issue of the relocation of Japanese-Americans in World War II. Such an issue remains relevant today since it highlights an inevitable clash of values in a democratic nation. It surfaced again in the outbreak of the war in the Persian Gulf as reporters clamored to have restraints on their access to information removed. The teacher's role at this point is to encourage students not only to express their views freely but to examine the grounds for their conflicting beliefs.

Step 3. Provide a background to the controversy. The teacher should encourage students to read their textbooks critically to determine if the author has dealt objectively with the issue or has slanted information one way or another. The teacher should suggest additional reading, including primary source materials (letters, diaries, documents, and photographs). Students may also view videotapes or films. Teachers should encourage students to make predictions before reading or viewing to build interest and encourage involvement.

Step 4. Increase the level of dissonance if appropriate. As students make predictions and read further, teachers may increase the dissonance level by providing for role playing or simulation activities in which students must make critical decisions on the issue. If students tend to avoid any involvement and cling to their own preconceived but uncritically examined beliefs, the teacher may need to introduce other views and information that challenge the students. For example, let us assume that students accept without question President Truman's decision to drop the atomic bomb on Japan in World War II–a decision that continues to be debated today. In this case, teachers might introduce students to William Caughlin's article in *Harpers* (1953), "The Great Mokasatsu Mistake–Was It the Deadliest Error of Our Time?" (Caughlin argued that the Japanese response to the Potsdam Declaration and the Allied demand for surrender was mistranslated as a refusal.)

Step 5. Reduction of dissonance and opportunity for further reading. Help students perceive the need for more reliable knowledge in grounding personal beliefs or making decisions. Some of the documents or reports introduced as evidence can be subjected to further scrutiny to determine reliability. Teachers should suggest that students strongly holding one view examine another position. Some students may find it helpful to gain a historical perspective on the issue. If the issue revolves around the clash between national security and the freedoms guaranteed by the Bill of Rights, students could examine the basis of Lincoln's difficult decision to suspend the writ of habeas corpus during the Civil War and more recently the case of *Tinker v. Des Moines Independent Community School District* in which students wearing black armbands to protest the Vietnam War were suspended from school.

Increasing evidence exists of the motivational force in the study of controversy. Shaver (1969, 34–49) concluded that emphasis on controversial issues would make the curriculum "more relevant to life." In the psychology of learning, the theories of cognitive dissonance and cognitive consistency lend credence to the idea that the carefully planned study of controversy can, in the words of Hunt and Metcalf (1968, 58), "lead to an awareness of inconsistency or conflict or inner conflict: it thus creates its own learning goal."

Summary

Social studies content lends itself quite naturally to enhancing the literacy abilities of students. The very social nature of social studies provides a natural vehicle to activating and using students' prior knowledge and developing metacognitive abilities. Teaching literacy skills through content areas is not a new concept. Only in the last decade, however, has research and practice given teachers a new direction for enhancing both literacy abilities of students and learning of social studies concepts through the use of learning strategies.

Motivating students is difficult at any level of schooling. As students progress through the grades, however, text difficulty and limited reading and writing ability seem to escalate the problem of motivation. Social studies content lends itself to the use of varied materials, realia, visuals, and controversial issues to build student motivation to learn. Other chapters of this book will offer additional learning strategies that can lead to increased desire on the part of students to become knowledgeable in the field of social studies.

References

Alexander, Mary. "Document of the Month: Photograph of a Land Auction." *Social Education* (January 1979): 30–31.

———, Ce. Ce. Byers, and Elsie Freivogel. "A Documentary Approach to Civil Rights." *Social Education* (November–December 1978): 563–581.

Allen, Rodney F. "The Critical Use of Tourist Brochures in World Geography Classes." *Journal of Geography* (February 1989): 6–10.

———, and Randall G. Felton. "The Use of Study Prints for Students of Florida History." In *Florida Council for the Social Studies: Annual Report, 1985–86.* Tallahassee, Fla.: Florida Council for the Social Studies, 1986.

Anderson, Richard C., Elfrieda H. Hiebert, Judith A. Scott, and Ian A.G. Wilkinson. *Becoming a Nation of Readers: The Report of the Commission on Reading.* Urbana, Ill.: The Center for the Study of Reading, 1985.

Armbruster, Bonnie B., and Thomas H. Anderson. "Producing 'Considerate' Expository Text: Or Easy Reading Is Damned Hard Writing." *Journal of Curriculum Studies* (January 1985): 247–263.

Background Notes on Botswana, U.S. Department of State. Washington, D.C.: U.S. Government Printing Office, 1990.

Baker, Linda. "Metacognition, Reading, and Science Education." In *Science Learning: Processes and Applications,* edited by Carol Minnick Santa and Donna E. Alvermann. Newark, Del.: International Reading Association, 1991.

Camperell, Kay, and R. S. Knight. "Reading Research and Social Studies." In *Handbook of Research on Social Studies Teaching and Learning,* edited by James Shaver. New York: Macmillan, 1990.

Caughlin, William J. "The Great Mokasatsu Mistake–Was This the Deadliest Error of Our Time?" *Harper's Magazine* (March 1953): 128–134.

Clark, Stephen. *The Complete Book of Baseball Cards.* New York: Macmillan, 1982.

Crofts, Marylee. "Africa." *Social Education* (September 1986): 345–350.

Davis, O. L., Jr. "Inquiring About the American Experience." In *Teaching about American History: The Quest for Relevancy,* edited by Allan O. Kownslar. Washington, D.C.: National Council for the Social Studies, 1974.

Derry, Sharon J. "Putting Learning Strategies to Work." *Educational Leadership* (February 1989): 4–10.

DeVries, Leonard. *Victorian Advertisements.* Philadelphia: J. B. Lippincott, 1968.

Dewey, John. *How We Think.* New York: Heath, 1933.

Erikson, Erik. *Childhood and Society.* New York: Norton, 1950.

Estes, Thomas H., and Joseph L. Vaughn. *Reading and Learning in the Content Classroom.* Boston: Allyn and Bacon, 1985.

Harvey, O. J., David E. Hunt, and Harold M. Schroeder. *Conceptual Systems and Personality Organization.* New York: John Wiley and Sons, 1961.

Herber, Harold. *Teaching Reading in the Content Areas.* Englewood Cliffs, N.J.: Prentice-Hall, 1970.

—————, and Joan Nelson-Herber. "Developing Independent Learners." *Journal of Reading* (April 1987): 584–589.

Hunt, Maurice P., and Lawrence Metcalf. *Teaching High School Social Studies.* New York: Harper and Row, 1968.

Jarolimek, John. *Social Studies in Elementary Education.* 8th ed. New York: Macmillan, 1990.

Kossack, Sharon. "NIE Week: ANPA–Resources for Reading." *Journal of Reading* (March 1987): 552–554.

Lunstrum, John P. "Building Motivation Through the Use of Controversial Issues." *Journal of Reading* (May 1981): 687–691.

Maslow, Abraham H. *Motivation and Personality.* New York: Harper and Row, 1970.

Mathison, Carla. "Activating Student Interest in Content Reading." *Journal of Reading* (December 1989): 170–176.

Moore, David W., John E. Readence, and Robert J. Rickelman. "An Historical Exploration of Content Area Reading Instruction." *Reading Research Quarterly* (Summer 1983): 421–438.

Mueller, Jean W. "Rock and Roll Heroes: Letter to President Eisenhower." *Social Education* (April 1985): 406–409.

—————, and Wynell B. Schamel. "Little House in the Census: Almanzo and Laura Ingalls Wilder." *Social Education* (November–December 1989): 451–453.

O'Neill, J. B. "A Primitive Economy." In *Strategies for Teaching Economics: World Studies Secondary.* New York: Joint Council on Economic Education, 1980.

Palincsar, Annemarie S., and Ann L. Brown. *Reciprocal Teaching of Comprehension-Monitoring Activities* (Technical Report No. 269). Champaign, Ill.: Center for the Study of Reading, 1983.

Reading Report Card: Progress Towards Excellence in Our Schools: Trends in Reading over Four National Assessments, 1971–1984. Princeton, N.J.: Educational Testing Service, 1985.

Sandler, Martin W. "How to Read Pictures." In *Improving the Use of Social Studies Textbooks,* edited by William Patton. Washington, DC: National Council for the Social Studies, 1980

Shapley, Barbara. "Law Studies and Newspapers." In *Florida Council for the Social Studies Report 1985-1986,* edited by R. F. Allen, F. I. Dorsett, and S. S. Day. Tallahassee, Fla.: Florida Council for the Social Studies, 1986.

Shaver, J. E. "Reading and Controversial Issues." In *A New Look at Reading in the Social Studies,* edited by Ralph Preston. Newark, Del.: International Reading Association, 1969.

Studying Societies: Patterns in Human History. City: Anthropology Curriculum Project of the American Anthropological Association, 1971.

Thelen, Judie. "Vocabulary Instruction and Meaningful Learning." *Journal of Reading* (April 1986): 603–609.

Tygiel, Jules. *Baseball's Great Experiment: Jackie Robinson and His Legacy.* New York: Macmillan, 1983.

Vernon, John. "It's in the Cards: Archives and Baseball." *Social Education* (February 1988): 124–126.

Yeaton, Connie S., and Karen Braeckel. *A Salute to the Constitution and the Bill of Rights.* Indianapolis: Indianapolis Newspapers Inc., 1986.

Chapter 2

Building Vocabulary and Conceptual Knowledge

Social studies teachers have the opportunity to develop and enrich the vocabulary and conceptual knowledge of their students. Content-area textbooks are replete with words and ideas more or less familiar to students. Some words have special meanings in social studies, and some words that teachers would expect students to know and be able to write can be troublesome to less proficient readers and writers.

Knowledge of vocabulary and concepts has been a topic under investigation for many years. In the last decade, research findings have identified some of the important factors in vocabulary and concept acquisition, thus permitting teachers to select instructional strategies to facilitate meaningful learning. Recommendations for vocabulary instruction have improved in the last decade because researchers now view vocabulary acquisition within the broader context of language and concept learning. They understand that vocabulary development is more than looking up words in a dictionary and writing sentences; rather, it involves the complex process of relating words to ideas or concepts.

"Vocabulary" and "concept" are difficult words to define because new understanding of learning has made the lines between them increasingly fuzzy. A student can have an extensive vocabulary which, of course, includes knowing the meanings of and fine distinctions between many words. It also means using a vast array of prior knowledge to understand concepts and relate them to each other. Vocabulary knowledge also encompasses the application of many subtle-

ties of our language and culture to understand the allusions found in jokes and idioms. For the purposes of this book, we will use the term "vocabulary knowledge" in the broadest sense to include conceptual knowledge. Because conceptual knowledge is particularly important to the learning of social studies content, we will present strategies that help students learn and relate concepts near the end of this chapter.

After a discussion of the importance of vocabulary knowledge, this chapter will also outline the various factors in vocabulary acquisition identified by researchers in the last decade. We will also include a discussion of the issues related to vocabulary instruction and a presentation of four guidelines for instruction. Finally, we will describe ways to develop conceptual knowledge using researched and field-tested learning strategies in the context of a unit of study.

The Importance of Vocabulary Knowledge

A wealth of research documents the strong relationship between vocabulary knowledge and academic achievement, specifically reading and listening comprehension. Anderson and Freebody (1981) hypothesized that vocabulary knowledge is strongly related to comprehension because: 1) understanding words enables readers to understand passages; 2) verbal aptitude underlies both word and passage comprehension; and/or 3) vocabulary knowledge may be related to a person's store of background information. Whatever the reason, we know that the proportion of difficult words in a text is the single most powerful predictor of text difficulty, and a reader's general vocabulary knowledge is the single best predictor of how well that reader can understand text. More simply put, people who do not know the meanings of many words are probably not proficient readers.

Nagy and Herman (1984) estimated that for students grades 4 through 12, a 4,500 to 5,400 word gap existed between low versus high achieving students. Others (Graves, Brunetti, and Slater 1982; Graves and Prenn 1986) found huge individual differences between high and low ability students. The findings were clear: high-achieving students know more words than do low-achieving students.

Until about 1950, the focus of vocabulary research emphasized four topics: 1) vocabulary size at various ages; 2) the relationship between vocabulary and intelligence; 3) identifying the most useful words to know; and 4) identifying a core of words that make text more understandable. In sum, most of the early research in vocabulary centered on choice of words to teach beginning readers and to implement readability formulas in the attempt to control text difficulty. Johnson (1986) predicted that the 1980s would be a period of rediscovering the importance of vocabulary instruction to reading comprehension. The promise was fulfilled.

The last fifteen years have yielded much high-quality research in language comprehension and production. It is only within the context of this research base that researchers and practitioners can understand vocabulary acquisition and make viable recommendations for effective instructional practices. Beck and McKeown (1990) contended that those interested in vocabulary acquisition must first understand the relationship between words and ideas, the role of inference, and the organization of information. Previous attempts to study vocabulary acquisition seemed fruitless until researchers achieved some level of understanding of the complexities of the mental processes involved in relating words to ideas.

Factors in Vocabulary Acquisition

Chall (1987) estimated that typical first graders understand and use about 6,000 different words. Most primary students understand thousands more words than they recognize in print; nearly all of these words represent concrete rather than abstract concepts. A shift in children's language takes place around age ten. The words they meet with increasing frequency after age ten are abstract rather than concrete, as they encounter concepts in social studies texts, abstractions in stories, and specialized content words in science. The research of the last two decades has helped to illuminate the complexity of the role of vocabulary instruction, but has left the resolution less clear. The first step in making decisions about effective and efficient vocabulary instruction is an understanding of various factors in vocabulary acquisition. These factors include: 1) what it means to "know" a word; 2) the role of context in incidental word learning; 3) the usefulness of definitions; and 4) the size and growth of vocabulary as a student matures.

Knowing Words

Beck, McKeown, McCaslin, and Burkes (1979) identified three levels of word knowledge: unknown, acquainted, and established. Suppose you ask a young child about different ways of measuring things in your home. You mention a "gauge" which she does not recognize (unknown). She recognizes "yardstick" as something to do with measuring, but would not be able to hand you one (acquainted). She has used a "ruler" in the past to measure her foot (established). Nagy (1985) contended that it takes more than a simple, superficial knowledge of words to make a difference in reading comprehension. That is, readers do not need to know all words in a text at the established level to comprehend what they are reading, but, for instruction of specific words to have an effect on reading comprehension, the understanding must be beyond a superficial level.

Blachowicz (1986) suggested the use of knowledge rating before reading to help students analyze their level of word knowledge (Figure 2.1). Before students read, the teacher presents a list of words related to the topic of study by placing a check mark along the continuum that reflects their level of knowledge of the word. The students analyze what they know about each word individually and then discuss the words they know or do not know and share information with each other. This activity leads naturally to preteaching vocabulary to be used later in the reading.

Figure 2.1

	known	acquainted	unknown
supply and demand			
production			
scarcity			
goods and services			

An issue related to knowing words is the importance of words in the text. Students apparently do not need to know all of the words in a text to understand it. Freebody and Anderson (1983) found that replacing one content word in six with a difficult synonym did not reliably decrease sixth graders' comprehension of text. Generally, students encounter text with 3 to 6 percent unfamiliar words. In sum, if the unfamiliar words are not important to the understanding of the text, students can tolerate a fairly large number of unknown words (about 15 percent) and still read with comprehension.

Context

Few would dispute the value of students' learning to use context to understand text and improve vocabulary growth. In light of recent research, however, a few caveats are warranted. Nagy (1988, 7) maintained that "context, used as an instructional method by itself, is ineffective as a means of teaching new meanings, at least when compared with other forms of vocabulary instruction." He contended that context rarely provides enough information for the person who has no other knowledge about the word. In another study, Nagy (1985) calculated that the probability of learning a word from a single encounter (in context) was between .05 and .11 with seventh and eighth graders. Herman, Anderson, Pearson, and Nagy (1987) found that higher reading ability and explicit text facilitated learning from context. The authors of these and other studies concluded that some learning from context occurs, but the effect is not very powerful. The reasons are emerging as researchers continue to investigate context as a vehicle for vocabulary growth.

Even considering these limitations, experts in vocabulary acquisition contend that the use of strategies to achieve maximum benefits from the use of context, even if the context is lacking richness, is still useful instructional practice, especially when teachers pair it with other learning strategies. After considering the dilemma, Nagy (1988) contended that a combination of definitional and contextual approaches is more effective than either approach in isolation.

Definitions

Used by itself, looking up words in a dictionary or committing definitions to memory does not lead to improved comprehension. This activity–a daily occurrence in hundreds of classrooms–leads only to a superficial understanding and rapid forgetting of a word. Two problems with definitions as a way to learn new words are: 1) often the reader must know a word to understand the definition, and 2) definitions do not always contain enough information for the reader to be able to understand and use a word. For example, a student finding "trade" as a definition for the word "commerce" is likely to write a sentence like "I will commerce my baseball for your goalie shirt." This sentence hardly captures the true meaning of "commerce." Reading comprehension depends on a deep understanding of the intent of the text, not merely on the definitional knowledge of the words contained therein. It appears, then, that the dictionary or glossary can best be used as a verification of meaning–that is, after the reader has a hunch as to the meaning of a word.

Educators must understand that learning a word involves more than lifting its meaning from context or reading its meaning in a dictionary. Rather, word knowledge involves a complex process of integrating new words with ideas that exist in the schema of the reader. Before we move to an extensive discussion of vocabulary instruction with specific teaching suggestions, one last factor in the vocabulary acquisition process is important to understand: the size and growth of vocabulary.

Size and Growth of Vocabulary

This factor has been a topic of long-standing debate. The number of words a person knows at any particular age depends on what an investigator counts as a word, with or without derivatives, and at what level a word is known. Nagy and Herman (1987) estimated that students learn approximately 2,700 to 3,000 new words annually.

A factor related to the size and growth of vocabulary involves the number of words available for exposure. Nagy and Herman (1987) analyzed the stock of words in school printed material in grades 3 through 9. They found that materials available for those grade levels contained approximately 88,500 words with upwards of 100,000 distinct meanings. Anderson and Freebody (1983) indicated that average fifth graders would be likely to encounter almost 10,000 new words a year while completing their normal school reading assignments.

Researchers have helped us understand that most children are capable of learning large numbers of new words per year. The question to raise is: where and how do students learn these words? Durkin (1978–1979) spent almost 300 hours observing fourth through sixth grade students and found that their teachers spent only 19 minutes of those 300 hours of instructional time in direct vocabulary instruction. Also, Nagy, Herman, and Anderson (1985) analyzed the number of words suggested in basal and content area textbook teacher's guides. They could attribute only 290–460 of the 3000 words that students learn each year to direct instruction. Nagy and Herman (1987, 23) concluded that "teaching children specific words will not in itself contribute substantially to the overall size of their vocabulary."

Although their belief is not held universally, Nagy and Herman (1987, 24) contended "that incidental learning of words from context while reading is, or can be, the major mode of vocabulary growth once children have really begun to read." They base their belief on previous studies (Herman, Anderson, Pearson, and Nagy 1987; Nagy and Herman 1987, 26) that indicated that reading grade-level texts produced a small, but statistically reliable, increase in word knowledge in grades 3, 5, 7, and 8 that were tested. The chance of learning a word from one exposure in text is somewhere around 1 in 20. They concluded, however, that "if students were to spend 25 minutes a day reading at a rate of 200 words per minute for 200 days out of the year, they would read a million words of text annually." With this amount of reading, children would encounter between 15,000 and 30,000 unfamiliar words and, if 1 in 20 of these words is learned, the yearly gain in vocabulary will be between 750 and 1,500 words.

Nagy (1988, 30) pointed out that very few people have experienced systematic, intensive, and prolonged vocabulary instruction, yet many adults have acquired an extensive reading vocabulary. People learn words from a number of sources, but "after third grade, for those children who do read a reasonable amount, reading may be the single largest source of vocabulary growth." In fact, Fielding, Wilson, and Anderson (1986) found that the amount of free reading was the best predictor of vocabulary growth between grades two and five.

Information about the size and growth of vocabulary is fascinating, but what are the implications for social studies teachers? Few educators would dispute the notion that reading leads to increased vocabulary growth. Reading in a content area such as social studies, which includes vocabulary from many fields (e.g., anthropology, geography, history, economics) is bound to enrich a student's vocabulary. Providing students with a wide array of reading materials related to the social studies unit can assist vocabulary growth in students. Systematic instruction in content areas, however, also leads to vocabulary growth. Some concepts need to be taught in a meaningful way to students, and words with special connotations in social studies need to be explored. In addition, the excitement of learning new words can be enhanced through social studies content.

Choosing Words for Instruction

Given that it is unlikely that students will learn a large number of words from direct instruction and given that instruction must be rich and extended, the words teachers choose for instruction are important. Graves and Prenn (1986) classified words into three types, each in succession requiring a higher investment of teacher and learner instructional time. The first type of word is one that is already in the student's oral vocabulary. Students merely need to identify the written symbol for this type of word. These words are generally mastered by the fourth grade, but poor readers continue to have problems with this type of word.

A second type of word is in neither the oral nor the reading vocabulary of the student, but can be easily defined through the use of more familiar synonyms. For example, although a student may not know the meaning of the word "altercation," this word can easily be defined by the words "argument" or "quarrel." Another type of word that fits into this category is a multiple-meaning word such as "bank," "run," or "bay." A student may know one meaning of a word but need a new or second meaning explained. It is estimated that one-third of commonly used words have multiple meanings. These multiple-meaning words are called "polysemous."

Polysemous words may be historically related. For example, students may know that the word "coach" means someone who guides a team. However, they may not know that a coach is also a vehicle. The new meaning can be traced to what people in medieval England called the person who drove the team of horses pulling the coach. The term was later applied to tutors in college, leaders of crew teams, and even later to anyone who guided a team as hard to handle as eight spirited horses. Polysemous words may also have a specific meaning in a content area. For example, all students know the word "change" as it relates to money. However, in social studies, "change" has a specific meaning somewhat different from our everyday sense of the word which may have to do with "changing societies" or "environmental change."

The third type of word is one for which the student has acquired no concept. This type of word is encountered frequently in the content areas. The teacher must take the time to develop the concept through instruction before students can understand the word. Words such as "scarcity" or "acculturation" are difficult concepts that are more readily understood after examples are given. Nelson-Herber (1986, 623) recognized the value of extensive reading to increase vocabulary knowledge, but maintained that "direct instruction that engages students in construction of word meaning, using context and prior knowledge is effective for learning specific vocabulary and for improving comprehension of related materials." Rich, direct instruction is necessary for teaching these difficult words.

Teachers may teach words that are already in the student's listening vocabulary through language experience activities or other writing experiences; however, multiple-meaning words and words embodying unfamiliar concepts need more direct instruction. In selecting words for instruction, teachers should consider them important for understanding a particular content area or to enhance general background knowledge.

Guidelines for Instruction
Help Students Become Independent Word Learners

If educators accept the premise postulated by Nagy and others that wide reading is the most effective vehicle for large-scale vocabulary growth, then helping students make the most of learning words independently is imperative. Carr and Wixson (1986) related this independence to the concept of strategic readers described by Paris, Lipson, and Wixson (1983). They suggested that readers should be responsible for learning a variety of methods to acquire word meanings (such as using context and structural analysis), have the ability to monitor their understanding of new vocabulary, and gain the capacity to change or modify strategies for understanding in the event of comprehension failure. Teachers discussing with some students how they figured out a meaning of a new word can help all the students. The more opportunities students have to use context and structural analysis and other strategies to guess the meanings of unknown words, they better they will become at that ability.

Encourage Active Involvement and Deep Processing of Words

What students do with newly learned words is more important than the number of words presented to them. Teachers can help students associate new words with what they already know through meaningful content or known synonyms. Students can learn how to make associations on their own in order to relate new words to their existing knowledge. Using new associations in writing and speaking is helpful to students. Direct instruction that engages students in the construction of word meanings by using context and prior knowledge has been found to be effective for learning specific vocabulary and important for the comprehension of related material (Nelson-Herber 1986).

Provide Multiple Exposures to Words

Students have a low likelihood of acquiring an adult understanding of a word from one exposure in a natural context (Nagy, Herman, and Anderson 1985). Many encounters with a new word are necessary if vocabulary instruction is to have a measurable effect on comprehension. If students are to retain words, the words must have meaningful usages in future reading and writing assignments. It seems logical that the introduction and use of new words should occur within a content area where reinforcement can naturally occur. An obvious cause-and-effect relationship is at work here: the more students are exposed to a word that occurs in a meaningful context, the higher the chance of students using and understanding that word.

Help Students Develop a Good Attitude About Learning Words Outside of the Classroom

Activities and gimmicks that help students identify, say, hear, or see words studied in class offer students repeated exposures in a meaningful context. These application exercises also help students strengthen the attitude that developing one's vocabulary is a lifelong process.

Teachers have found the following strategy helpful when they develop a list of 3–5 words for the week. They make a list of these words and tape it to the corner of their desks for referral. The teacher attempts to use each word five times during the week and tallies each time he or she uses one. Eventually, the teacher tells the students what he or she is doing and why ("I am trying to increase my vocabulary"). Soon, the students imitate the teacher's behavior, copy his or her list, and try to use the words also. Some students make up their own lists. However the details of the activity work out, the clear message is that learning new words is a lifelong process.

Foster Extensive Reading Outside of Class.

Wide reading facilitates large-scale vocabulary growth. Teachers should encourage students to read outside of class. Sustained silent reading times, giving students lists of books, and using the media center are all good ways of encouraging wide reading beyond the classroom walls.

A Sample Unit: The Ancient Chinese and Demonstrated Learning Strategies

The major thrust of this chapter thus far has been on vocabulary knowledge in its broadest sense. Because learning concepts is central to the understanding of social studies content, we have chosen learning strategies to demonstrate that teachers can integrate language learning into the enhanced learning of social studies concepts. Language arts and reading teachers use these strategies widely; many content area teachers have also found them useful. The special value of this approach is that students increase their conceptual knowledge while enhancing their learning of social studies content.

Suppose a social studies teacher is about to begin a unit on China. The new unit words suggested in the textbook for instruction are: dynasty, pictographs, character, mandarin,

Mandate of Heaven, jade, civil service, and porcelain. After reading the particular selection, the teacher determines that these additional words might be unfamiliar to students: chariot, nomad, and millet.

The major concepts to be learned in this selection are that: 1) dynasties were predominant among early civilizations; and 2) early Chinese writing, based on symbols called pictographs, eliminated all but the wealthy and educated people from positions of power, since writing was a prerequisite for rulers.

Earlier in this chapter, we made two important points that can help a teacher decide which words merit extensive treatment and which should be treated lightly or ignored. The first point is that some words are more important than others for students to understand the text. The second point is that teachers must consider the extent of student prior knowledge when making decisions about vocabulary instruction as explained with the three types of words. Below is an example of the decisions made relative to the unit on the Ancient Chinese:

a. "Dynasty" is an important concept and necessary for understanding the text; needs preteaching.

b. "Character" is a high utility word and also polysemous (type two word). The word has other meanings that teachers should explore first to help students make the connection.

c. "Mandate of Heaven" and "civil servant" are important concepts for understanding the selection and need some preteaching.

d. "Jade," "porcelain," "chariot," "nomad," "millet," "mandarin," and "pictograph" are words that are incidental to understanding the text. Teachers should reinforce their meanings in post-reading activity.

The activities presented below are samples of ways to develop vocabulary related to a particular reading or topic. Most likely, a teacher would choose among these activities, depending on the prior knowledge of students and

LIBRARY
UNIVERSITY OF ST. FRANCIS
JOLIET, ILLINOIS

teaching objectives.

These learning strategies are used widely in classrooms and are flexible enough to fit a variety of content. We chose these particular strategies because they help students become independent word learners, encourage active involvement by having students relate new words to previously learned concepts, provide multiple opportunities to use new words through reading, writing, speaking, and listening activities, and encourage students to use words in new contexts outside the classroom.

List-Group-Label

Taba (1967) first developed the List-Group-Label Strategy as part of her Concept Formation Model. Teachers can also use this strategy as a diagnostic instrument to discover what students know about a subject and as an organizational tool to facilitate higher-level thinking. Since the strategy involves categorizing and labeling words, List-Group-Label makes an excellent prereading strategy for vocabulary development lesson as well.

Step 1: The teacher elicits from students as many words as possible related to a particular subject. The teacher may use a variety of stimuli: show a picture, read a story, show a film, give a lecture, or display artifacts or objects. Pictures of China from the textbook or other sources may evoke responses such as farmer, rice, pagoda, people, very old, rickshaw, bicycle, chop suey, Great Wall, and gun powder. The teacher may also elicit words by asking students to brainstorm what they know about a particular topic. We generated the sample list below by showing students pictures of China.

rickshaw	*chop sticks*	*kings*
bicycle	*kimono*	*very polite*
farmers	*dynasty*	*sons*
poor	*rulers*	*paddies*
pointed hats	*Buddha*	*books*
rice	*porcelain*	*Confucius*
tea	*silk*	*vases*

Step 2: The teacher helps students group related items by asking students which words could go together to form a group. Students may note that items may belong to more than one group. After students determine appropriate categories, they group words accordingly. One type of marking system is shown below:

Step 3: The teacher helps students give a label to each group. After students have grouped related items, the teacher asks them to label each group of related words. The list below shows a marking system to identify the labels or concepts identified.

Taba's model extends this initial phase of categorizing into Interpretation of Data. To encourage students to think at higher levels, the teacher would ask them to compare observations of Ancient Chinese civilization with what they know about life in China today. Students could then be asked to identify similarities and differences. Furthermore, the students would be asked to make generalizations about the similarities and differences noted. In the third phase, Application of Generalization, students would apply the generalization to a new situation and examine what would happen if they applied the generalization. To continue our example, after the List-Group-Label activity about China, the students may form the generalization that "China is radically different than it was because of a change in government." The students then may be asked to apply this same statement to a new situation by considering the question, "What changes will occur in the next 100 years?"

Educators have used the Taba Model as a means of promoting concept development, higher-level thinking, and developing vocabulary knowledge in students for four decades. This activity provides motivation through opportunity for success. All students can participate by sharing with the class their perceptions of a picture. Students can then develop higher-order thinking skills through categorizing, interpreting, and making generalizations. Students also learn words by grouping them logically and in a way that makes sense to them. By examining examples of a concept and grouping them, students learn new vocabulary as they are exposed to the labels other students apply.

Word Maps

Although students may not know much about dynasties, they are familiar with the television show "Dynasty." Also, they know some things about rulers, kingdoms, monarchs, and presidents. Word maps can take many forms. Here is an example of one word map for "dynasty." Teachers can add as much or as little structure as the students need to build background for a particular concept.

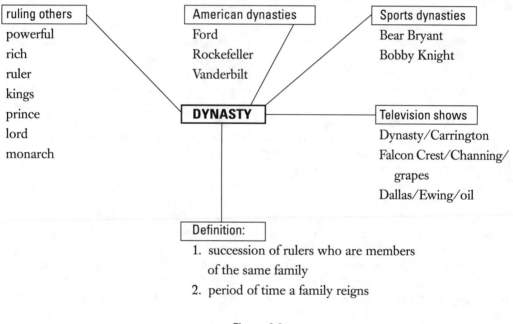

Figure 2.2

Word maps can be more open-ended. For example, if a student (or class or group) constructed a word map of "character," the polysemous nature of the word would soon become evident. For students to gain a deeper meaning of the word, the relationship between the Chinese "character" and the person "character" would add a richer meaning to both words.

Capsule Vocabulary

The unique feature of the Capsule Vocabulary is that it incorporates all four language areas into the process of building vocabulary. Crist (1975) originally developed this strategy to improve the vocabulary skills of college students in a language lab. It has been successfully adapted for use in middle and secondary school classrooms. Some teachers choose to use review words from previous units to give students an opportunity to read, write, speak, and listen to the capsule words. The steps comprising this strategy are illustrated by using the topic "dynasties."

Step 1: The teacher prepares the capsule. A group of words related to a particular topic is identified. These words can come from a previously studied chapter or a new topic. The list of words is handed to the students. For "dynasty," the following words were chosen:

dynasty	*kingdom*
monarch	*authority*
colleague	*potentate*
ruler	*dominion*
family	*generation*
noble	*emperor*

Step 2: The teacher introduces capsule words. Teacher and students engage in a ten- to twenty-minute discussion on the topic using as many of the capsule words as possible. The students try to identify these words. As each word is identified, it is checked off on their list of words and defined if necessary. If the teacher or students are uncomfortable with the discussion format, a written format may be used as suggested by Cunningham, Cunningham, and Arthur (1981). This format consists of a paragraph containing the words. The students underline the capsule words found within the paragraph.

Step 3: Students practice using the words as part of their speaking/listening vocabularies. Students are placed into small groups where they have their own discussions. The teacher instructs them to use as many of the new words in a conversation as possible and record with a tally system when they use each word.

Step 4: Students practice using the words in writing. The final step is to have the students write. Students can write themes, dialogues, or stories about the topic, again using as many new words as possible. The writing can be done by individual students or in cooperative writing groups.

Many educators agree that using all four language systems reinforces learning. This strategy provides students with an opportunity to speak new words, read new words, listen to others use the new words, and finally write those new words in a meaningful context. One young woman in Crist's (1975, 149) original pilot group summarized the experience by saying: "It's cool–or I should say, 'gratifying'–to be verbose."

Contextual Redefinition

One of the most important aspects of helping students become independent vocabulary learners is helping them to use context effectively. The use of context allows readers to make predictions about unknown words and then to verify those predictions using syntactic and semantic clues. Contextual Redefinition (Cunningham, Cunningham, and Arthur 1981) is a strategy that introduces new vocabulary in rich contexts. These contexts help students to define words and facilitate the retention of these words.

Step 1: The teacher selects words she thinks will be unfamiliar to students. These are words that may be troublesome to students but are important for understanding of the passage.

Step 2: The teacher presents the words in isolation. The teacher asks the students to provide a definition for each unfamiliar word. Some guesses may be funny or "off the wall," but the teacher should accept these guesses in the spirit of guessing. For example, students may guess that "Mandate of Heaven" means finally getting a date with the person of their dreams. Or "civil service" may mean a wedding in which everyone is polite. After the guessing period, students are asked to reach consensus about the meaning of the word.

Step 3: The teacher presents a sentence that illustrates the meaning of the unknown word. If such a sentence exists in the text, that sentence should be used. Different types of context clues such as contrast or synonym should be used to accustom students to making use of such clues. Following are sentences that could be helpful to students attempting to determine the meanings of "Mandate of Heaven" and "civil service":

The Chinese people supported each new ruler because of what they called the "Mandate of Heaven." They believed that the king or emperor who gained power had been selected by heaven to rule.

T'ang emperors developed an examination system for government officials that was used for centuries. This system established "civil service." In the civil service system, government officials were selected based on their qualifications rather than on noble birth.

Using these contextually rich sentences, the teacher then asks students to try to guess the meanings of the new words. Students should be asked to provide a rationale for their guesses because it is helpful for students to hear the thought processes of others.

Step 4: Students use the dictionary to verify guesses. The teacher asks a student to look the word up in the dictionary or glossary to confirm the guesses of the class.

Contextual Redefinition not only provides an opportunity for students to learn new words but it assists them in becoming independent word learners through the use of context clues. After this activity, students will probably realize that trying to guess at a word's meaning in isolation is frustrating and often futile. Also, as mentioned earlier, students benefit from being actively involved in predicting and confirming word meanings. Finally, the proper role of the dictionary or glossary is emphasized throughout this activity–that of verifying guesses as to word meaning.

Assessing Vocabulary

After the reading, the meanings of some less important words may be reinforced. Below is an example of a post-reading activity.

1. Which of these would you _____?
a. read	1. millet
b. ride	2. jade
c. eat with	3. chariot
d. wear	4. pictograph
e. eat	5. porcelain

2. Could a "nomad" be a "mandarin"? Why or why not?

The teacher may reinforce these words by asking students to use them in a writing activity or asking students to find the words in speaking, listening, reading, or writing experiences outside the classroom. This type of activity helps students use words in a meaningful context and leads them toward a more sophisticated understanding of words.

Summary

Educators, for some time, have recognized the important role of vocabulary and conceptual knowledge in comprehending text. Researchers in the last decade have pointed the way to improving the effectiveness of instruction in this area. Recent investigations in the richness of context in natural text, the usefulness of text, the level to which a person "knows" a word, and the size and growth of vocabulary and concepts helped educators understand that the acquisition of a full, rich, and functional vocabulary involves the complex process of relating words to ideas.

Experts in the field of language development agree that the main vehicle for instruction should be encouraging students to read widely. Selected words, however, should be chosen for extended, rich instruction. This instruction should focus on helping students become independent learners, encouraging students to become actively involved in the processing of selected words, providing multiple opportunities to use words, and guiding students to develop a good attitude about learning words outside the classroom. Research-based and field-tested learning strategies such as List-Group-Label, Contextual Redefinition, and Mapping are available for teachers at any level to use. Along with wide reading, these strategies help students learn unfamiliar words by associating words to be learned with ideas and words they know.

References

Anderson, Richard C., and Peter Freebody. "Reading Comprehension and the Assessment and Acquisition of Word Knowledge." In *Advances in Reading/Language Research: A Research Annual,* edited by B. Hutton. Greenwich, Conn.: JAI Press, 1983.

————. "Vocabulary Knowledge." In *Comprehension and Teaching: Research Reviews,* edited by John T. Guthrie. Newark, Del.: International Reading Association, 1981.

Beck, Isabel L., and Margaret G. McKeown. "The Acquisition of Vocabulary." In *Handbook of Reading Research,* edited by P. David Pearson. 2nd ed. White Plains, N.Y.: Longman, 1990.

Beck, Isabel L., Margaret G. McKeown, Ellen S. McCaslin, and A.M. Burkes. *Instructional Dimensions That May Affect Reading Comprehension: Examples from Two Commercial Reading Programs.* Pittsburgh: Learning Research and Development Center, University of Pittsburgh, 1979.

Blachowicz, Camille L. "Making Connections: Alternatives to the Vocabulary Notebook." *Journal of Reading* 29 (April 1986): 643–649.

Carr, Eileen, and Karen K. Wixson. "Guidelines for Evaluating Vocabulary Instruction." *Journal of Reading* 29 (April 1986): 588–595.

Chall, Jeanne S. "Two Vocabularies for Reading: Recognition and Meaning." In *The Nature of Vocabulary Acquisition,* edited by Margaret G. McKeown and Mary E. Curtis. Hillsdale, N.J.: Erlbaum, 1987.

Crist, Barbara I. "One Capsule a Week: A Painless Remedy for Vocabulary Ills." *Journal of Reading* 19 (November 1975): 147–149.

Cunningham, James W., Patricia M. Cunningham, and Sharon V. Arthur. *Middle and Secondary School Reading.* New York: Longman, 1981.

Durkin, Delores. "What Classroom Observations Reveal About Reading Comprehension Instruction." *Reading Research Quarterly* 14 (December 1978–January 1979): 481–533.

Freebody, Peter, and Richard C. Anderson. "Effects on Text Comprehension of Different Proportions and Locations of Difficult Vocabulary." *Journal of Reading Behavior* 15 (1983): 19–39.

Graves, Michael F., Gerald J. Brunetti, and Wayne H. Slater. "The Reading Vocabularies of Primary Grade Children of Varying Geographic and Social Backgrounds." In *New Inquiries in Reading Research and Instruction,* edited by Jerome A. Niles and Larry A. Harris. Rochester, N.Y.: National Reading Conference, 1982.

Graves, Michael F., and Maureen C. Prenn. "Costs and Benefits of Various Methods of Teaching Vocabulary." *Journal of Reading* 29 (April 1986): 596–602.

Graves, Michael F., and Wayne H. Slater. "The Development of Reading Vocabularies in Rural Disadvantaged Students, Inner-City Disadvantaged Students, and Middle-Class Suburban Students." Paper presented at the meeting of the American Educational Research Association, Washington, D.C., April 1987.

Herman, Patricia A., Richard C. Anderson, P. David Pearson, and William Nagy. "Incidental Acquisition of Word Meaning from Expositions with Varied Text Features." *Reading Research Quarterly* 22 (Summer 1987): 263–284.

Johnson, D. D. "Introduction: Vocabulary." *Journal of Reading* 29 (April 1986): 580.

Nagy, William E. *Teaching Vocabulary to Improve Reading Comprehension.* Newark, Del.: International Reading Association, 1988.

————. "Vocabulary Instruction: Implications of the New Research." Paper presented at the meeting of the National Council of Teachers of English, Philadelphia, PA, November 1985.

————, and Patricia A. Herman. "Breadth and Depth of Vocabulary Knowledge: Implications for Acquisition and Instruction." In *The Nature of Vocabulary Acquisition,* edited by Margaret G. McKeown and Mary E. Curtis. Hillsdale, N.J.: Erlbaum, 1987.

————, and Patricia A. Herman. "Limitations of Vocabulary Instruction" (Technical Report No. 326). ED 249 498. Urbana, Ill.: Center for the Study of Reading, 1984.

————, Patricia A. Herman, and Richard C. Anderson. "Learning Words from Context." *Reading Research Quarterly* 20 (Winter 1985): 233–253.

Nelson-Herber, Joan. "Expanding and Refining Vocabulary in Content Areas." *Journal of Reading* 29 (April 1986): 623–626.

Paris, Scott, Marjorie Y. Lipson, and Karen K. Wixson. "Becoming a Strategic Reader." *Contemporary Educational Psychology* 8 (1983): 293–316.

Taba, Hilda. *Teacher's Handbook for Elementary Social Studies.* Reading, Mass.: Addison–Wesley, 1967.

Chapter 3

Using Reading and Writing to Foster Critical Thinking

Critical thinking has continued to command the interest and attention of social studies teachers at all levels over a number of decades. Curriculum designers justify emphasis on critical thinking by pointing out that children and adolescents are literally bombarded with misleading and unreliable messages in both the electronic and print media. Moreover, since the central goal of the social studies has long stressed the development of skills required of citizens in a democracy with particular emphasis on decision-making, it follows inescapably that critical reading should be an essential component of social studies instruction. After leaving school, students, as citizens, must face a wealth of choices as they approach such basic decisions as buying a car, deciding on marriage (or divorce), supporting a political candidate or cause, and advancing their own views in both the public and private sectors. In virtually all cases, they must find a way to scrutinize printed information and derive reliable knowledge to serve as a basis for action.

Often the term "critical thinking" is used as a synonym for critical reading and writing. Indeed, it may be said that critical thinking encompasses critical reading since critical thinking, as Russell (1956) observed some time ago, involves at least four basic processes:

1) Acquisition of knowledge of the areas in which the thinking occurs.
2) A disposition to assume an attitude of questioning and restraint on hasty judgments, i.e., reflecting before accepting.

3) Employment of a method of scientific inquiry and/or logical analysis.
4) Carrying out a plan of action derived from these processes.

Devine (1986) summarized succinctly the relationship between critical thinking and critical reading in these words: "When readers think critically about and with the printed page they may be said to be reading critically" (251). The major focus of this chapter is on the development of sound content-related strategies to strengthen critical reading and writing. First, we discuss the nature of critical reading and other language skills and then analyze significant aspects of recent research on critical reading in the social studies. Next, the chapter moves to an explanation of a theoretical framework to guide the integration of critical reading and writing into the content and process of teaching social studies. The first major component of this framework is what has been termed a foundation comprised of two major elements: 1) the creation of a teaching/learning climate to facilitate the introduction and application of critical reading/writing strategies, and 2) the introduction and frequent classroom application of the inferencing process.

The second major component of the framework treats in detail seven basic strategies that comprise (in the view of reliable authorities in the field) the process of critical reading. Examples throughout the chapter show how teachers may integrate the strategies into the content of the social studies.

Critical Reading and Other Critical Language-Processing Skills

Writers such as Hennings (1986) and Devine (1989, 296) pointed to a significant relationship between critical reading and critical listening. "Many teachers have found," explained Devine, "that lessons in critical reading have become more effective when combined with instruction in critical listening." Although Devine focused his concern on the elementary school, a good case can be made for linking instruction in critical reading and critical listening in the secondary school.

Other writers have investigated the importance of critical viewing, particularly with reference to television, and have called for more emphasis on this approach to offset the miseducative aspects of the extensive pattern of television viewing so characteristic of many adolescents and children. In a comprehensive review of the research on mass media with particular implications for instruction in social studies, Splaine (1990) underscored the pervasive power of this electronic medium and pointed to examples of the negative effects of excessive television viewing, particularly with reference to a number of issues including the "compression of information" in reporting political news, the treatment of women and minorities, and violence portrayed as problemsolving. Concluded Splaine (1990, 397), "How teachers can work with parents to help children develop critical viewing and listening skills is a major challenge."

A close relationship between reading and writing has been noted consistently in research. Early (1984, 200) found that "an excellent way to learn critical reading is through writing oneself." An assumption made explicit in this chapter is that reading and writing are "mutually reinforcing language acts," to borrow an apt phrase from Early. Hence, critical reading cannot be taught effectively without provision for the development of writing abilities.

Research on Critical Reading as Related to the Social Studies

In a recent comprehensive analysis of research dealing with reading in the social studies, Camperell and Knight (1990, 575) expressed doubts about the efficacy of traditional skills-based instruction in critical reading in the social studies. They noted a high degree of resistance to critical reading in the social studies as readers "tend to distort the meaning of a text to conform to preexisting knowledge." They also cite literature that demonstrates that readers are "extremely tolerant of ambiguities, inconsistencies, and untruths in passages they hear or read." Camperell and Knight finally concluded that the ability to read critically is a "late-emerging skill," which rests upon an essential knowledge base, an understanding of the students' own reading strategies, the ability to comprehend the organizational structure of texts, and instruction on how to evaluate written materials.

We do not share Camperell and Knight's pessimistic prognosis suggesting that we must resign ourselves to waiting for the appearance of a "late emerging skill." Clearly, educators concerned with pressing demands of citizenship education can ill afford the luxury of waiting for critical reading skills to emerge while their students, unable to discern bias and misleading illogical arguments, run the risk of becoming easy prey to skillful propagandists. It may be conceded that barriers have existed to effective instruction in critical reading in the social studies. A number of studies (Gagnon 1989) of social studies textbooks have emphasized the bland, sterile treatment of content often divorced from the reality of meaningful controversy. Other studies have shown that social studies teachers have not previously chosen to provide direct instruction in comprehension in their classes (Batson 1982; Smith and Feathers 1983). Notwithstanding these findings, two assumptions appear warranted: 1) the barriers to effective instruction in critical reading are not insurmountable, and

2) strategies to develop critical reading have never been integrated into the content and instruction of social studies in a meaningful fashion.

Building a Foundation for Critical Reading
The Classroom Climate

Early (1984) advanced a proposal for a unit on student self-assessment of performance as critical readers. This proposed unit is not intended to replace any instruction in critical reading but rather to make the critical reading process more meaningful. Early's proposal can serve three purposes in the social studies: 1) helping students become aware of the ways authors can sway their views or appeal to their emotions; 2) encouraging students to acquire the skills needed for critical examination of both the print and electronic media; and 3) providing opportunities in these self-assessment units to practice the critical reading skills acquired in the course. This assessment technique can often be simply one class period and can also contribute to an atmosphere in which students feel free to raise issues, question what the author of the text says, state opinions, and explore the foundations of those opinions.

Here is how a self-assessment unit might work in a social studies class. At an appropriate, logical point, the teacher introduces an issue related to some aspect of the subject under study. It should be on a topic on which one might expect marked differences of opinion among students. It might be on the legalization of marijuana or the rights of gays to teach or freedom of the press in wartime. The teacher selects the article (possibly an editorial or letter to the editor of a local newspaper) supporting or opposing a principle held dear by the students. The students read the article silently or listen to a reading by the teacher, after which the teacher reads statements designed to focus on biases implicit in the material. The

students reflect their opinions by displaying cards indicating "agree," "disagree," or "don't know." The teacher may also introduce the task of rapid reading of short statements containing deliberate errors of fact to see how skillful students are in perceiving the inaccuracies and correcting them.

After students become aware of the way in which their biases or perspectives influence their comprehension, the teacher should then help the students analyze the article paragraph by paragraph to help them arrive at an understanding of what the author is saying and what purpose the communication served. Early has recommended helping students apply a model originally proposed by Lasswell in the 1930s for critical analysis of communications. The model, although somewhat dated, still has the advantage of promoting awareness of the receiver (understanding of self) and awareness of the sender as indicated in the following:

Who. Who is the communicator, the author? What are his or her qualifications, background, etc.?

Said What. What did the author say? (Accurate comprehension should be stressed.)

To Whom. What audience is the target of the message? How does it affect the message?

Through What Channel (i.e., radio, newspaper, etc.). How might this affect the content of the message or the language used?

With What Effect. Was the message reportorial (factual) in style or emotive or biased?

How well did the author succeed? How justifiable is the purpose of the communication, according to an evaluation in terms of the reader's, listener's, or viewer's values?

For teachers preferring a more comprehensive, structured model encompassing the basic elements of the Lasswell model, the reading checklist proposed by Thistlewaite (1990) is recommended. This checklist includes questions to help the student examine the following: authority of the writer; bias or objectivity of the writer; purpose and attitude of the writer; up-to-dateness and validity of the material; use of reasoning and support; and bias and objectivity of the reader. Thistlewaite also provided a useful model for critical reading of editorials.

In building a climate of open-mindedness in the classroom through self-assessment, the process of writing is also recommended as reinforcement. Teachers may encourage students to respond in writing to deep concerns they have about an issue by writing a letter to an elected official or the editor of the local paper or forwarding a petition to some official. Some examples of provocative issues that typically have roots in the social sciences are: ecology, pollution, law enforcement, drug control, and human rights.

The self-assessment approach is suitable for middle school and secondary school, although teachers could also use it with some modifications in the upper elementary grades. The approach would be most effective if used in the introductory part of the course and incorporated periodically at appropriate intervals through the course as a guided practice or application procedure.

Making Inferences

Popularly defined by some as "educated guessing," researchers nevertheless view inferencing in literacy education as fundamental to most reasoning activities. Devine (1986, 231) says unhesitatingly that inferencing is the one skill that "seems to predominate in all mental activity." Some research literature now sees inferences as "slot-filling" activities, i.e., filling in gaps by predicting the missing information on the basis of other clues present. It might happen in a social studies class when students viewing an unlabeled artifact in a museum or on a field trip identify correctly the function of the artifact from its structure and size and on the basis of their own experience.

Goodman (1984, 105) and Devine (1986, 233) both see the process of inferring as the "general strategy of guessing on the basis of what is known and what information is needed but not known." Yet Goodman cautioned that using the word "guessing" to describe inferencing does not make the process mysterious or intellectually sloppy: "Our schemata and knowledge structures make it possible on the basis of partial information to make reliable decisions by inferring the missing information." He reminded us that "we would be incapable of the decisions we must make if we had to be sure of all of the necessary prerequisite information before making each decision" (105). Yet endorsing inferencing as an essential skill in critical thinking carries with it the responsibility for helping students distinguish inferences from facts and opinions and learning how to evaluate inferences.

Some students may initially need additional structure in developing and practicing inferences. In that case, a Predictions Guide such as that developed by Nichols (1983) may provide a useful example from U.S. history, as shown in the sample Prediction Guide in Figure 3.1.

Questioning Strategies and Inferencing

Questioning strategies used by both teacher and students play an essential role in developing skill in inferencing and critical thinking. Effective questioning may help the teacher determine if students have the background to comprehend the assignment and identify areas where students are confused and lack prerequisite knowledge. Teachers may use several useful approaches to encourage inferencing with questioning. A fairly simple model for social studies teachers to incorporate in their courses for both print media and visual materials is that of Klein (1988) who proposed an approach called PTC for Predict-Test-Conclude (Figure 3.2).

FIGURE 3.1. SAMPLE PREDICTION GUIDE

Part A. Directions: Before reading the chapter, see how well you can predict what you are going to learn. Draw on what you have read thus far about the Articles of Confederation and the background to the calling of the Constitutional Convention. In Column **A**, place a check next to each statement you believe will be proven true in the chapter.

A   B

__   __   1. Before the Constitution was written, the states made most of the laws.
__   __   2. There was only one kind of paper money in the U.S. before the Constitution.
__   __   3. The Constitution will contain guarantees for freedom of press, freedom of
               religion, and freedom of speech.
__   __   4. The Constitution will outlaw slavery.

Part B. After reading the chapter, put a check in Column **B** by all statements you believe are true. How much did you improve your understanding from your reading?

Part C. Rewrite each sentence that is not correct to make it agree with the text. You may use your textbook.

FIGURE 3.2. PTC APPROACH

Prediction Phase (prereading)

1. In this first phase, the teacher develops at least three questions to help students hypothesize about likely events or outcomes in the text or related materials.
2. The teacher should provide activities or other questions to bring out the students' background knowledge–in short, to draw on their schemata. An overview, diagram, or an advanced organizer might help. Also helpful would be to preteach difficult vocabulary terms to show how the words are used in context.
3. Students are next asked to write down their predictions based on responses to the teacher's questions and their reading of the overview or the initial passages of the materials. The students can use these predictions in the next phase (the reading phase) as they read to test their hypotheses and to reconstruct them if warranted.
4. Students discuss the written predictions and foundations for them.

Reading Phase

1. In the reading phase, the teacher may provide suggestions with clarifying statements and questions to guide the reading, particularly in classes where a large number of students may have reading difficulties.
2. The teacher should monitor individual progress by circulating around the room, responding to individual student questions.

Post-Reading Phase

The teacher discusses with the students the accuracy of their predictions (inferences), and then probes to see what support they found for their predictions, determine where students did not adequately support inferences, and suggest ways for improving the process of inference-making. The teacher should ask students to verbalize the operations they used to arrive at the inferences. The teacher will ensure that they revise or restructure poorly grounded inferences. Questioning may begin in this phase at higher reasoning levels and relate to the original hypotheses students generated. If necessary, teachers should use lower-level, probing-type questions to elicit recognition of information overlooked. As an option, the teacher may ask students to summarize what they learned from the exercise.

Here is an example to show how the PTC model might work in a government class that has been discussing energy policies in the United States. Copies of the following passage from a journal might be distributed to the class or it might be placed on a transparency and projected on a screen:

Wednesday, March 28, Camp Hill, Pa. Coming home from the grocery store I hear the news bulletin of a minor problem at reactor #2. Having long felt uneasy with the concept of nuclear energy, I think, "Damn, here we go again. . . ." (Teachers will find Nancy Austin's "Diary of Three Mile Island Incident" in *Social Education,* October 1979.)

This kind of unstructured discovery-type approach can stimulate interest. The teacher can ask students about the kind of a document this is. (Most will recognize it as a diary or log.) Then students can go on to determine if the word "reactor" has meaning for them. Ask someone to check the location of Camp Hill, Pennsylvania, and speculate on who might be writing this. A nuclear technician, a politician, a reporter? A teacher may then pose the question, "What do you think is going to happen in this account as you read further?" and encourage students to express ideas and probe for the foundations of their inferences. The teacher may ask them to anticipate the major ideas or issues the writer will treat in the diary as they read it in its entirety. At this point, the teacher distributes the remainder of the diary for study and reading during phase two of the PTC.

It is important to use appropriate strategies to ensure that the majority of students have access to the schemata needed for a basic understanding of the content and related concepts. In view of the variety of differences in students' linguistic and experiential backgrounds, this is an essential first step.

In the third phase (post-reading) of the PTC strategy, the teacher would ask students to share their predictions with the class, recognizing the tentative nature of such hypotheses. The teacher would encourage students to question one another as to the bases of their speculations about what may have happened and what might transpire next. If students hesitate, the teacher might ask where the event occurred and what additional information they need. Some students might confuse the 1979 Three Mile Island incident in Pennsylvania with the 1986 disaster at Chernobyl in the Republic of the Ukraine (formerly part of the Soviet Union). In this event the teacher may choose to introduce accounts (available in most encyclopedias) comparing the two nuclear accidents, describing the causes and effects on the population and the environment.

If time permits, students may investigate the political and economic implications of both nuclear accidents in the United States and Russia. On the subject of nuclear safety and the future of nuclear energy, the students may contrast arguments of organized groups supporting expansion of nuclear power with opposing views particularly from environmentalists. As a concluding activity, students working in groups reflecting differing views may compose letters stating their convictions with supporting evidence to be sent for publication as letters to the editors of local newspapers.

Critical Reading Viewed as the Development of Essential Strategies

Considerable consensus exists among writers in the field (Devine 1981; 1986) that seven strategies represent the process of critical reading (and are closely related to the strategies prescribed for critical listening and viewing). Briefly stated, these are:

1) Recognize the purpose(s) of the author in the written communication.
2) Distinguish relevant from irrelevant information.
3) Evaluate the sources.

4) Take note of special points of view.

5) Distinguish fact from opinion.

6) Recognize and evaluate inferences.

7) Recognize biased, slanted, and emotional language.

In the remainder of this chapter, we will present instructional strategies and activities based on the foregoing list of skills. Teachers may introduce these strategies into the existing social studies program without a significant reorientation of teaching methods or content. Also to be identified are appropriate sources of information containing ideas and strategies that teachers may readily incorporate into the curriculum to build critical reading and writing skills.

Recognizing the Author's Purpose in Communication

Discovering an author's purpose may appear a prosaic task, but some students simply have never reflected on an author's purpose and how it may affect the content of the message. In analyzing purpose, teachers must alert students to two possible levels of purpose: the explicit, public purpose, and the hidden or less obvious purpose.

Using Posters. A simple way to introduce this skill is to focus attention on posters containing bold visual images, with words or slogans where the author's or artist's intent is clear and forthright. Many history texts or supplementary materials will contain varied posters reflecting the national spirit and issues in critical periods. Examples of World War I posters in vivid colors may be found in *American History Illustrated* (1988, 32–45). Such posters clearly reflect a wartime call to arms for the military or to mobilize civilian support. The purposes are clear and explicit. A less public purpose may be to create heroic images of the military and build public confidence in wartime. To facilitate the development of this strategy, it may be helpful to write on the board possible

choices in identifying the purposes of the posters at both the public and hidden level. Teachers can encourage students to select what they consider the best statement of purpose and to defend their choices. Teachers can then follow up with an explanation of the clues to look for in identifying the author's (artist's) purpose.

A somewhat more demanding and intriguing task is to analyze the poster, focusing on the subject of the African-American soldier in World War I (Bodle 1985). The poster shows an African-American family looking up at a large picture of a uniformed man who is obviously their father. Below the large picture are two smaller pictures of George Washington and World War I president, Woodrow Wilson, resting on the mantle above the fireplace where a large log is blazing, filling the room with a feeling of security and comfort. To the right and above the picture of the soldier surrounded by small American flags is a picture of Abraham Lincoln. At the bottom of the poster are two words: "True Blue." (The poster obtained from the National Archives is available as a color foldout in *Social Education,* February 1985.)

Teachers will need to develop some background about the state of race relations in the United States and the sometimes-overlooked role and treatment of the African-American soldier in war at the time. (The poster would be particularly helpful as an inquiry-oriented springboard in a U.S. history course when dealing with World War I.) Because the poster is vivid and rich in use of symbols, it provides an opportunity to arouse interest and to frame probing questions such as the following: What is happening in this scene? Who are these people looking at in the picture? What is their relationship to the black soldier whose picture is displayed on the wall? What does the term "True Blue" mean? Why was this poster produced and distributed? What feelings does it seem to inspire? What purposes do you think it was intended to serve?

Using Letters. Primary source materials such as posters, letters, logs, and cartoons can not only enrich an often less-than-exciting textbook, but in most cases materials from the National Archives can be reproduced for classroom use within the constraints of copyright laws. A letter such as that from Eleanor Roosevelt, wife of President Franklin Roosevelt, to the President General of the Daughters of the American Revolution (DAR) (Freeman, Bodle, and Burroughs 1984) can focus attention on a significant event in the evolution of race relations in the United States, a process often neglected in texts. The text of the letter (available from the National Archives) is reproduced below.

February 26, 1939

Dear Mrs. Robert:

I have never been a very useful member of the Daughters of the American Revolution, so I know it will make very little difference to you whether I resign or whether I continue to be a member of your organization.

However, I am in complete disagreement with the attitude taken in refusing Constitution Hall to a great artist. You have set an example which seems to me unfortunate and I feel obliged to send in to you my resignation. You had an opportunity to lead in an enlightened way and it seems to me your organization has failed.

I realize that many people will not agree with me, but feeling as I do, this seems to me the only proper procedure to follow.

Eleanor Roosevelt

Roosevelt's letter at first glance contains a recognizable purpose: she resigned from the DAR because that influential, patriotic orga-nization, influenced by the then-prevailing Southern attitudes on segregation, denied use of its great hall to an internationally famous African-American singer, Marian Anderson. She clearly states in her letter that she is in complete disagreement with the action taken, but more subtly she hints of another less apparent purpose when she writes, "I realize that many people will not agree with me." She had undertaken a bold act of private conscience, unprecedented for a First Lady. She deliberately broke and in so breaking challenged the then firmly established rules of race relations in this country. In the aftermath of her action, she was the victim of scurrilous attacks in the Southern press, and very few white people came to her rescue. But among African-Americans at that time, her declaration of conscience brought new hope. In the words of Walter White, then NAACP president, her action "focused worldwide attention on the episode" (Lash 1971, 685). Available to teachers in *Social Education* (Vol. 8, No. 7) are copies of Mrs. Roosevelt's letter (curiously unsigned), a copy of the reply from the DAR, and some suggested teaching activities.

Distinguishing Relevant from Irrelevant Information

After students have learned to recognize the two levels of the author's purpose, they need to understand that authors may at any time inject into their messages information that is not relevant or does not bear on the major topic or theme. This may occur deliberately to distract the reader from a possible flaw in the author's reasoning or to mislead the reader; or it may be simply accidental.

Elementary students can learn that, if the author's purpose in an article is to encourage travel to a Latin American country, he or she will not introduce information relating to the dangers of hijacking on airlines unless, as Devine (1981) pointed out, there is a hidden reason for doing so. Teachers can alert older students to the introduction of irrelevant information in the form of logical fallacies. One particular dangerous fallacy to recognize which may appear in political messages is called argumentum ad hominem (literally translated from the Latin, "attack the individual"), in which the speaker or writer will divert attention from a real issue by launching a personal attack on an opponent using labels such as "liberal free spender" or "fascist." To introduce this skill, the teacher may give students lists of items most of which relate to major themes or issues, and ask students to cross out those that do not belong under a given theme or topic. Then the teacher may select editorials or letters to the editor as practice exercises for students and ask students to detect various ways in which irrelevant information is injected into the articles.

Evaluating Sources

Students should have an opportunity to learn very early that authors and speakers may lack the competence to speak or write about the subjects they have chosen. For an introduction to this problem of judging sources on the basis of qualifications in the elementary schools, Devine (1981) suggested giving students mixed lists of topics and authorities and inviting them to match the topic with the authority. Initially, the jumbled lists should contain easily recognizable names of sports figures, rock stars, and TV or movie personalities, along with topics or occupations where a mismatch is unlikely. Later, the teacher may convert this activity to a social studies activity for older students by listing, for example, such historical personalities as Eli Whitney, Susan B. Anthony, Thomas Jefferson, Frederick Douglass, Robert E. Lee, Ulysses S. Grant, and Chief Seattle. Topics to be matched with a given author might include a variety of subjects such as slavery, invention of the cotton gin, Declaration of Independence, or women's suffrage. Some students might be challenged to explain why Frederick Douglass would make a more competent author concerning slavery than, say, Thomas Jefferson, who deplored slavery but still owned slaves. Douglass, as students should learn in the investigation, was an escaped slave who later bought his freedom, and eventually became an influential writer and orator in support of abolition during the Civil War period.

Teachers should encourage middle and high school students to check on reported authorities (political figures, experts on foreign policy) who express vigorous views on controversial issues and claim attention in the press. To stimulate student interest in evaluating sources, teachers can cite historical and contemporary examples of individuals who claimed power and authority and have written widely about critical issues on the basis of very dubious credentials. For a recent example, one can point to Saddam Hussein, the Iraqi president, who claimed on the basis of very flimsy credentials to be a great military leader and then proceeded to lose his war against allied forces.

In the United States, we might look at the records of powerful demagogues in this country who have shaped history on the basis of very dubious backgrounds. There is the case of D. C. Stephenson, a Texas drifter and con man who became Grand Dragon of the Indiana Ku Klux Klan and, as such, more powerful than the governor of the state during the national resurgence of that sinister organization in the 1920s (Rissler 1966). Stephenson distributed literature widely proclaiming the great mission of his organization to save the United States from what he saw as internal perils. Then there was the case of the part-time life insurance salesman and minister, Sidney Catts (dubbed by one historian as the "Cracker Messiah"), who became Governor of Florida in an upset election in 1916 largely by writing and talking about an alleged Catholic conspiracy to seize control of America and by demanding that convents be inspected for concealed supplies of arms (Flynt 1977). More recently, we have witnessed human tragedies, abuses of power, and serious financial losses stemming from the ill-founded claims to expertise and power by cult leaders such as Jim Jones and David Koresh. As studies of demagoguery and roguery suggest, it appears that all too often the magnetic personality and the power to move and cultivate people may carry more weight with some people than reputable credentials.

When evaluating sources, secondary school students need to learn to ask the critical questions: What are the qualifications of this person? Does she or he have wide experience in the claimed field of expertise? Does the author or speaker have the necessary educational background? To this list of inquiries, Devine (1986, 252) suggests checking on the background of the individual for a "hidden reason for speaking and writing on the topic." Students should learn to use reference books in the library to check on an author's or speaker's background; these might include *Who's Who*, biographical dictionaries, encyclopedias, and almanacs. A useful exercise might be to provide students with excerpts of some of the writings of a selected number of prominent demagogues (at appropriate points in a history, sociology, or government course) and ask them to evaluate the sources by checking qualifications. Finally, we should remind students regularly that printed texts and literature are not sacred documents, that they were written by human hands, and "consequently, are sometimes incorrect, sometimes biased and sometimes deceitful" (Devine 1981, 105).

Readers and listeners experienced much frustration in repeated reports of the imminent release of the hostages in Lebanon from "highly placed sources" in a terrorist organization. (Reliable journalists reporting this development made it clear that it must be taken with the proverbial grain of salt.) Special cautionary advice to students is in order at times. Students must learn to listen, view, and read reports with great caution and skepticism when those reports emanate from sites where

there is press censorship or evidence of intent to manipulate the news. Concern has been expressed about the Gulf War reporting from Baghdad by Peter Arnett of Cable News Network (CNN). Critics contended that CNN expressed no clear warning that Arnett was reporting the news under conditions of strict press censorship in the Iraqi capital. Transcripts of U.S. newscasts and special documentaries can usually be obtained from networks. Students may then study the transcripts and collect data on the source. They may also compose letters to news organizations critical of the use of dubious sources of information or to defend, for example, reporters like Arnett, who struggle despite strict censorship to get the news out.

Taking Note of Special Points of View

To introduce this strategy, a good beginning might be to examine letters to the editor where the writers' points of view are made abundantly clear. The editorial pages of most daily papers feature letters reflecting a broad range of topics. Letters stressing points of view are also found in the national news magazines such as *Time* and *U.S. News & World Report*. Sometimes comparing headlines of different newspapers can reveal an unmistakable point of view. Compare for example these two headlines dealing with the same story on the same day:

November 28, 1965 New York Daily News
PEACENIKS PARADE IN D.C. & NOTHING MUCH HAPPENS

November 28, 1965 Chicago Tribune
WHITE HOUSE PICKETED BY 12,000 IN PROTEST OF VIETNAM POLICY

Also helpful in arousing interest in the concept of point of view are the reviews of current movies that often differ in their appraisal of various films. As a case in point, there was general popular and critical acclaim for the movie *Glory*, which was about an African-American Union Regiment (the 54th Massachusetts Infantry) in the Civil War. However, one reviewer in an African-American newspaper, the *Washington Informer*, had some deep reservations (Steele 1990). *Glory*, said its headline, "Raises Many Questions." Members of the 54th Infantry comprised largely of freemen "are not revealed as rational thinking beings in *Glory*," said reviewer Ronald Steele. Questioning why the white commander, Colonel Shaw led his men to a hopeless assault (and slaughter) on Ft. Wagner, Steele indicts the movie as biased: "To European Americans, *Glory* may be a great movie but to this African American it is blaxploitation." It might be interesting and instructive to students who have seen the movie to compare a favorable review with that of Steele's.

To reinforce instruction in recognizing points of view, students might be asked to write letters to the editor on current issues expressing a point of view considered consistent with a role they assume. They might take an issue that surfaced in the Gulf War about peace demonstrations and respond orally or in writing to the question, "Are peace demonstrations undermining the morale of our troops?" Students might assume the roles of the following: a confirmed peace activist from the Vietnam era, the mother or father of a soldier or marine in the Gulf, a disabled and disillusioned Vietnam veteran, and an attorney belonging to a civil libertarian organization.

Students may later present a roundtable discussion in which each presents a different point of view on a controversial issue, following which the class may speculate on and analyze factors that may have contributed to the points of view expressed. In history and government classes, teachers and students may organize a reenactment of important decisions reached in U.S. domestic and foreign policy over the years. Some decisions might include: President Truman's decision to fight in Korea, the Cuban missile crisis in the Kennedy era, the Supreme Court decision of *Roe v. Wade*, and Lincoln's decision to issue the Emancipation Proclamation despite opposition from border state leaders and a number of Northern politicians. After some research into the actual events and parts played by various individuals in the Cabinet, the Supreme Court, National Security Council, the Congress, and special interest groups, students can assume roles to present and defend their points of view in simulated sessions chaired by the presiding officer of the appropriate organization.

Combining Strategies. Teachers can readily use two strategies–Recognition of Points of View and the Evaluation of Sources–in combination. To accomplish this, students can analyze history books written 10 to 20 years apart and note differing points of view We may also observe, as Smith (1990) suggested, that the names of African-American, Hispanic, and women leaders have been added to recent historical accounts. The interpretation of a major historical event may have changed owing to more recent historical research. A case in point is the post-Civil War reconstruction period termed many years ago by Claude Bowers the "Tragic Era," an era supposedly characterized by northern brutality, excesses, and corruption. A key feature of this thesis was the abuse of power by former slaves placed in political office by Yankees to punish poor southerners. (This southern theme of exploitation and martyrdom was popularized in such early movies as *Birth of a Nation* and novels such as *Gone With the Wind*.) More recent historical research reveals a far different picture, with much of the violence coming from southern white vigilante groups (Shofner 1974) and constructive political reform efforts undertaken but later aborted as northern troops were withdrawn from the South.

Yet another example that provides a timely

opportunity for students to apply skills of recognizing a point of view and evaluating sources is that of the case of the explorer Christopher Columbus. Earlier portraits of Columbus portray him as "one of the greatest souls that ever lived . . . a man of lofty intellect, of wonderful enthusiasm and of deep religious nature" (Allen, Swett, and Royce 1889, 74). Today, after the Quincentenary of the Voyage of Columbus, we draw on the insights of contemporary, critical students of history and we perceive for the first time another side, a dark side, to Columbus. He is now portrayed by some as a man responsible for bringing devastation, disease, disaster, and slavery to thousands of Native Americans (Crosby 1987; Jennings 1975). Students may examine conflicting points of view about Columbus and write brief position papers to explain how we should view Columbus and what role we should assign to him in history.

Students need to grasp the idea that our view of history is changing and unfolding as our values and beliefs change and our knowledge base expands. What should emerge from activities such as those described above is an understanding of how the purpose of authors and their points of view and information sources are shaped by what historians call *zeitgeist*, the intellectual, moral and cultural climate of an era.

Comparing two or more conflicting accounts of the same event can also be the focus of combined strategies development, i.e., perceiving the author's purpose, noting the special point of view, and evaluating the source. When considering the concepts of colonialism and imperialism in Africa in world history, students have an opportunity to focus on combined skill development in the story of Stanley and Mojimba and their encounter on the Congo River. In one of the great news events of the late nineteenth century, Stanley (1885) was the famous reporter and explorer in search of a missing medical missionary, Livingston. Mojimba, a king in the Congo

River region, having heard of Stanley's coming up the Congo sought to welcome the explorer (by his own account later recounted to a German missionary) but instead found himself and his men in the middle of a battle.

Seeing King Mojimba's large war canoes bearing down on him amid loud shouting and a "swelling barbarous chorus," Stanley (1885, 268–269) reported that he advised his men: "Boys, be firm as iron, wait until you see the first spear, then take good aim." Mojimba's account (Schiffers 1957, 197) asserted his peaceful intentions and expressed anguish over what he saw as an unprovoked attack. As Mojimba explained it, "We swept forward, my canoe leading, the others following with songs of joy and dancing, to meet the first white man our eyes had beheld and to do him honor. But as we drew near his canoes there were loud reports, bang, and fire staves spat bits of iron at us."

Guidelines for Evaluating Primary Sources. As students examine the preceding examples of conflicting accounts of the same event, teachers should carefully instruct them on four special guidelines to follow in evaluating primary sources of information (and to be considered in some secondary accounts):

1. Information given in a primary source may be more or less biased because of the differing abilities of the witnesses and participants to observe and report events accurately. Ethnocentrism, social pressures, and personal interests limit observers' ability to report events accurately.

2. Information given in primary sources may be more or less biased due to the intent of the writers. To be more specific, if the document was written only for the writer's eyes (as is the case of a personal diary), it is probably more reliable than a source written for a large audience. When the writer, or the witness to a major event, expects a large number of people to read his or her account, the writer may try to influence the

readers to accept a particular point of view.

3. Information given in primary sources may be more or less biased according to the qualifications of the writer. In general, the rule is that the more expert the observer, the more reliable his or her account, unless there is reason to believe that bias exists in the form of a predilection for one position over another.

4. Information in a primary source may be more or less reliable depending on the amount of time that has elapsed between the event and the reporting of it. If some time has elapsed before the account is set down on paper, the observer of or witness to an event may become confused or forget essential details. When two or more accounts differ markedly and both accounts are equally flawed for one reason or another, readers may analyze both to see where there is agreement on any elements in the account and/or then seek a more reliable third source.

Distinguishing Fact from Opinion

Even some adults have difficulty applying this skill (Devine 1981). Clearly, this is a basic part of critical thinking; in fact, some teachers may prefer to teach it along with the skill of drawing inferences to preclude the possibility that students may conclude that an unsupported opinion is a legitimate inference. For young children, a necessary foundation skill to distinguishing fact from opinion is the ability to differentiate between the real and the imagined (Burns, Roe, and Ross 1982). It is recommended, therefore, that elementary teachers help children master this skill. Some authors suggest having children change a factual account into a fantasy by incorporating such elements as talking animals and magical events. This should not discount fantasy as unworthy or untrue, but given the power of special effects in the mass media and the cinema, a very real danger exists that some children will remain unable to separate the real from the unreal.

Teachers should remind students periodically that factual statements are verifiable by someone other than the reader and that opinions express feelings, unsupported beliefs, and preferences. One way to introduce this skill is shown in Figure 3.3, a sample or model exercise that might be appropriate in a history or government class studying campaigns and elections.

On occasion, students can and should debate the differences between fact and opinion. The distinction is by no means clear even to logicians (Devine 1981). However, the point of this sample exercise (and others similar to it) is to provide the opportunity for students to question the claims they frequently hear, read, and view about what is established factual information. They should be encouraged to evaluate, reflect, and critique. After the introduction and initial practice in applying this skill, students should bring to class examples of opinions and facts drawn from advertising in the mass media, newspaper editorials, and even textbooks. Teachers may use a prediction activity or guide to introduce an assignment in social studies classes by listing in jumbled fashion factual statements and statements of opinion by textbook authors or from primary source materials included in the text. Students should first predict which statements are facts and which are opinions, and then read their assignments to verify or correct their responses. Discussion may then follow to address any problems students have had in making distinctions.

Recognizing and Evaluating Inferences

After students have learned to distinguish fact from opinion, a next logical step is to recognize and evaluate inferences. We have suggested the importance of inference-making and some ways for testing inferences. However, the process of thinking critically requires a greater understanding of how poorly grounded inferences may mislead readers and

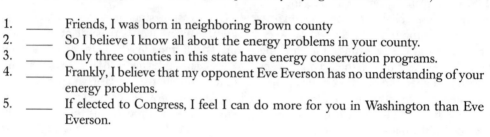

Figure 3.3. Model Exercise: Critical Listening

Candidate for Congress John Johnston made a campaign speech recently to the Chamber of Commerce, broadcast over radio and television and published in a local newspaper. A part of his speech is reproduced for you to examine. You are to indicate in the appropriate blank whether the statement is a fact or opinion by placing the letter "F" for fact or "O" for opinion in the appropriate blank. Facts are statements of concrete information that may be proven. Opinions are statements that express personal feelings, beliefs, and preferences. (Sometimes a person will offer an opinion by saying "I think" or "I feel.")

1. _____ Friends, I was born in neighboring Brown county
2. _____ So I believe I know all about the energy problems in your county.
3. _____ Only three counties in this state have energy conservation programs.
4. _____ Frankly, I believe that my opponent Eve Everson has no understanding of your energy problems.
5. _____ If elected to Congress, I feel I can do more for you in Washington than Eve Everson.

encourage them to accept an unwarranted position. An example that comes to mind is that of the report of finding arsenic in the strands of Napoleon's hair sometime after his death on St. Helena in May 1821. From that single fact, an inference was stretched to support a conspiracy theory that Napoleon had been poisoned (Phillips 1974). Students should note that, no matter how intriguing a conspiracy hypothesis, only one piece of evidence in this case is offered in support of it. As Phillips noted, the hypothesis is lacking in certainty since with some imagination one could conceive of additional evidence that would turn up later to render the hypothesis less probable than before.

In the case of great personalities in history or contemporary leaders, it is tempting for some to infer that a conspiracy has occurred to order the data to explain a troubling event, such as a death or disaster. This process of stretching an inference is seen in the literature on the assassination of President Abraham Lincoln. Barzun (1990) recalled that Secretary of War Stanton kept Major Thomas Eckert, a formidable bodyguard, from accompanying Lincoln to Ford's Theater on that fatal night; Stanton also dissuaded General Grant from joining the Lincoln party. From those occurrences, some writers, notably Otto Eisenschiml, a professional chemist, have inferred that Stanton was at the heart of a conspiracy with the Radical Republicans to kill Lincoln since they feared his opposition to their views on Reconstruction. Eisenschiml's views, which were published in the late 1930s, attracted much public attention (Epperson 1991), although professional historians were generally critical. Historians have pointed out that there are other reasonable explanations for Stanton's actions not taken into account in Eisenschiml's conspiracy hypothesis.

One does not have to look far beyond today's headlines to find other evidence of the need for careful evaluation of inferences. Reports regularly appear in the press hinting about secret deals and assassination plots. This caution is not to recommend outright rejection of such inferential speculation but rather to caution students as they search for alternative viable explanations in unearthing the sources of information. As recent history shows in the case of Watergate, careful investigation of facts and the inferences drawn from them have led to some significant findings that have dramatically changed the course of events and affected many people.

Recognizing Biased, Slanted, and Emotive Language

Teachers can take several approaches to sensitize students to the uses or misuses of language to distort, mislead, or persuade. In this section, we focus on three approaches: analysis of linguistic factors, propaganda analysis, and doublespeak.

Linguistic Factors. Linguistic factors such as choice of words and phrases or use of the passive voice may be employed by authors or speakers with intent to influence readers or listeners or to persuade them to accept an unexamined point of view or set of values or to purchase a product. To introduce this skill in critical thinking, the teacher might ask students to react to the following two statements. Neither is false, but one is intended to influence opinion more than the other:

1. The candidates were George Henderson, president of United Electronics, and Esther Lunsford, a pert, blond grandmother of five.
2. The candidates were George Wilson, president of United Electronics, and Esther Lunsford, a Certified Public Accountant.

Discussion may center on such questions as: Which statement is more appropriate for Esther Lunsford? What bearing does the description of Esther as "a pert, blond grandmother" have on her candidacy for office? Students should see these comments about her appearance or family relationships in this context as irrelevant and sexist. Teachers can probe to see if students understand why.

To help the class recognize the uses or misuses of what some call "loaded words" (Devine 1986), the teachers can explain to students that meaning may be conveyed subtly by a choice of synonyms for a key word. Some synonyms are positive, conveying a favorable impression;

some are negative, conveying an unfavorable image; and others are neutral or simply factual. One way to begin is to note both negative and positive words and phrases drawn from an editorial on a controversial topic or from a letter to the editor in a newspaper expressing a strong point of view on a topic of local interest. Ask students what feelings they experience and what emotions, values, or beliefs the words or phrases imply. Here is a list from a recent newspaper editorial on Hiroshima on the occasion of the anniversary of the dropping of the atomic bomb on that Japanese city: Holocaust, horror, distorts the truth, treacherous destabilization, alternative, nuclear age, bloodshed, earth.

A teacher can explain to students that these words appeared in an article about Hiroshima, making sure all students grasp the significance of Hiroshima and asking students what feelings, emotions, or beliefs are aroused by the connotations of the words and phrases. Then, discuss the basis for their reactions. Not all students may experience the same reaction. Indeed some may experience no negative or positive reactions, possibly because they are unable to access a schema for Hiroshima or the atomic bomb. If that is the case, the teacher can probe to find out why.

For an approach that is sure to elicit some response, write on the board "police officer" and ask students for synonyms. Group their responses under the categories negative, positive, and neutral. The teacher may then show students how euphemisms (after explaining the term) may be used to create a detached, neutral image. Military briefings held during the Persian Gulf war offer other examples of euphemisms, such as "strategic withdrawal" for "retreat," "collateral damage" for "civilian casualties," and "target rich environment" for "many potential bombing opportunities." Other possible sources are the public statements of state and national legislators and other elected officials and government agencies. Some euphemisms are relatively amusing and harmless such as "urban transportation specialist" for a taxicab driver. But others, such as "destabilizing a government" for illegal overthrow of a legitimate government, are dangerous because they alter our perception of reality (Lutz 1988). Ask students to be alert to uses of negative and positive synonyms and applications of euphemisms in the electronic and print media and to bring examples to class. As noted later in this chapter, the use of euphemisms can be analyzed also within the framework of doublespeak analysis.

In teaching students how to recognize efforts to use linguistic factors to mislead, misinform, or deceive, the research literature recommends two basic teaching plans. One, the emphasis on recognition of propaganda devices, has apparently had more appeal in social studies, whereas doublespeak has seemingly been more widely applied in English classes. The following paragraphs explore the potential of both approaches for more effective application in the social studies.

Propaganda Analysis. The interpretation of critical thinking as the detection of propaganda devices (e.g., "bandwagon" or "testimonial") has a long history dating back to the work of the Institute of Propaganda Analysis (IPA) in the 1930s (Smith 1974). A number of studies have suggested that even students in the intermediate grades can learn to detect the presence of propaganda techniques not only in textual materials but also in the mass media (Smith 1974; Wardell 1973). A widely favored classroom exercise using this approach is to have children study advertising and determine what devices advertisers use to influence buyers. Then, having perceived the uses of the devices, ask them to write their own propaganda-laden commercial messages. Listed below are seven of the typically used devices:

- *Glittering generality*–noting a vague broad statement loaded with words having positive connotations and ignoring the exceptions to it.

- *Name calling*–giving something a bad label, thus calling attention away from the issue.
- *Transfer*–trying to make the prestige and authority of something transfer to another.
- *Testimonial*–linking the prestige of one person to something quite different.
- *Plain folks*–making a person, especially a star or a politician, appear to be just like everyone else.
- *Bandwagon*–saying that everyone else is doing something; therefore, you should do it, too.

Gunther, Martin, Maxwell, and Weiss (1978) expanded this list to include other devices such as appeals in various forms to tradition, authority, large numbers, and popular passions. This analysis appears to be helpful as Gunther and others demonstrated in proposing analysis of documents having political and social significance to detect devices; then, students are asked to write messages incorporating propaganda devices for a good cause. This exercise may strike some as being of dubious value, but we may counter any objections by assigning to other students the task of critiquing and rewriting the propaganda-laden messages. These authors show how it is possible to apply their expanded list of propaganda techniques to the analysis of an official Ku Klux Klan document.

Doublespeak. Doublespeak analysis as a procedure for teaching critical thinking is somewhat more recent in origin. It stems from the work of the 1975 Committee of Public Doublespeak of the National Council of Teachers of English, which launched what has now become a movement among teachers of English. The committee on doublespeak recognizes annually the dubious achievements of organizations in their employment of doublespeak. "Doublespeak," explains Lutz (1988, 41), "is not the product of careless language or sloppy thinking. Indeed, most doublespeak is the product of clear thinking and is language carefully designed to communicate when in fact it doesn't. It is a language designed not to lead but mislead."

Although the doublespeak movement does not seem to have had much influence on teaching social studies thus far, it has drawn on the talents of a number of thoughtful writers in the field of linguistics (Rank 1976; Stanley 1976), and it clearly deserves a hearing by social studies educators and practitioners. Particularly worth noting in this connection is Rank's (1976, 4) rejection of the popular IPA classification scheme previously described. Not only does this pattern of analysis of language of 1930s vintage make "intrinsic errors of classification," but Rank concluded, "The list [of propaganda devices] simply doesn't have the scope or flexibility to deal with contemporary propaganda." In its place, Rank has proposed a two-part schema focusing on the intensification of language by the techniques of repetition, association, and composition and the downplaying of language through omission, diversion, and confusion (Rank 1976). In the following, we show the two-part schema and explain the techniques used by writers to produce doublespeak. The task of the reader is to recognize how these techniques are used and to reject false misleading information, thus requiring the users of doublespeak to desist and communicate with greater clarity.

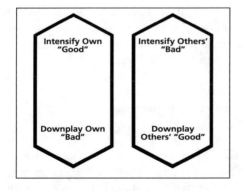

Figure 3.4 Diagram of Doublespeak
Based on Hugh Rank. "Teaching About Public Persuasion: Rationale and a Schema." In *Teaching About Doublespeak*, edited by Daniel Dietrich. Urbana, Ill.: National Council of Teachers of English, 1976.

Doublespeak has one significant advantage that should appeal to social studies practitioners. Not only does it carry the endorsement of reputable students of language, but it can also provide a broad framework for teaching several critical thinking skills in combination and reinforce learning through guided practice. One example in the form of a model doublespeak/critical thinking activity is based on an editorial, "Hiroshima: Let That Be Our Last Holocaust" (*Tallahassee Democrat*, August 6, 1986, 8), and letters to the editor commenting on the editorial. (This editorial can be used effectively by teachers and students in history classes when they are studying World War II.) The purpose and point of view of the writer seem to be to denounce America's use of the atomic bomb in World War II, and to warn that continued development of nuclear weapons can result in another and greater holocaust. A brief scenario follows to show how students may apply the doublespeak strategy.

It may be assumed in the absence of any identification that a member of the editorial staff wrote the editorial, and students would be able to get in touch with the newspaper for further information on the background and qualifications of the writer or writers. (One can infer some views of the writer from an announcement inserted in the editorial about the Tallahassee Peace Coalition holding a Hiroshima Day vigil.) The writer uses rich emotive and slanted language to underscore the broad appeal for peace. President Reagan is charged with using "deceptive numbers when urging the abandonment of the SALT II treaty and resisting a nuclear test ban treaty." The result, the author assures us, is a "treacherous destabilization of the superpower standoff which could ignite at any time into the holocaust that Hiroshima foreshadowed."

The writer also questioned American motives for using the atomic bomb on the assumption that large Allied casualties could be avoided. Downplaying the issue of high cost in casualties, the editorial writer states that the highest estimate for casualties of the Joint War Plans Committee at the time was 40,000 American lives, according to Barton J. Bernstein, a Stanford University professor of history. Here we can observe the author's inferential leap from Professor Bernstein's statement to the conclusion that "the truth was bent" for "after the fact justification." (Question: Who bent the truth, and what is the evidence?) The implication seems to be that the loss of 40,000 American lives is not a serious issue—again the theme of downplaying. (Question: Who is Professor Bernstein? What are his credentials in this field other than being a professor of history at Stanford? That alone does not make him an authority on the issue being examined.) For the reader, there are certain unfortunate omissions of important information needed to make an objective evaluation of this assumption that "the truth was bent." (Note how doublespeak analysis calls attention to omissions of data that might weaken the writer's position and how the writer uses words and the picture of Hiroshima to intensify the language supporting the writer's position.)

Teachers may ask students to research Professor Bernstein in *Who's Who* and other sources, and then ask students who else would make a good authority. How about the Allied Commander on the scene in World War II? Who was he, and what did he have to say? Teachers might then suggest that General MacArthur's estimates and views be examined and compared with Professor Bernstein's. A reliable and readily available source of information on MacArthur is William Manchester's prize-winning biography, *American Caesar* (1978, 510-514). Students who investigate will find the following pertinent information:

1. General Douglas MacArthur, Supreme Commander in the Pacific, estimated in a letter to Defense Secretary Stimson in 1945 that "Operation Downfall," the code name for the invasion of Dai Nippon, would cost one million American lives.

2. MacArthur based his estimate on intelligence reports indicating that the Japanese were prepared to resist to the last, using women and children in addition to the over 30 million Japanese soldiers on the home islands including regular troops, prison troops, and civilian militia (the number of available Japanese troops exceeded at that time the combined armies of the United States, Great Britain, and Nazi Germany).

3. MacArthur had also been fighting the Japanese for four years and knew the fighting abilities of the Japanese soldier and his fanatic devotion to his emperor.

Before reaching any final conclusion, students will need to gather information to evaluate the source cited in the editorial. In evaluating sources, caution students that reports written about a significant event after a substantial time lapse are less reliable than those written at the time. Before concluding the exercise, encourage students to debate this question: Is one ever justified in using doublespeak to advance one's views? Are the editorial pages of the newspaper or programs on television (such as "Crossfire") appropriate forums for the employment of doublespeak? As a concluding activity, students might be asked to write a response to the editorial they have scrutinized, using clear unambiguous language and avoiding the pitfalls of doublespeak.

Summary

In this chapter, we have emphasized showing how teachers can infuse the basic strategies of critical reading into the content of the social studies. In the lower elementary grades, teachers should encourage children to differentiate between reality and fantasy. As they move to the upper elementary level, children should be encouraged through discovery-type activities to begin to draw inferences that in turn may contribute to their ability to acquire skill in recognizing the author's purpose in a communication, whether a folktale or an editorial. Observing how writers use words to communicate an idea, to persuade, to obscure, or to mislead is a skill that can be introduced in upper elementary levels and then reinforced and extended in the middle school and high school levels. Finally, at appropriate points in the middle school and high school curriculum, students can acquire skill in scrutinizing both secondary and primary source materials while they probe the validity of the communication and assess the reliability of the communicator.

The major thesis of this chapter is that critical thinking–a major goal of the social studies–is simply not attainable unless there is direct, repeated instruction (linked to meaningful content) in ways to scrutinize the printed message and to assess the validity of claims made by authors of texts, politicians, and all who wield influence or authority in a democratic system. Citizens must have the knowledge and skill in oral and written communications to hold accountable those to whom they have given the power to make decisions. The social studies class must serve as a forum for examining and testing competing ideas expressed in the print media.

Some critics might argue that such an emphasis on combined content and skill development will produce a generation of cynics and skeptics estranged from their government. To this, we can reply that the loyalty of a free people to their nation is assuredly not derived from civic passivity and political alienation nourished by the confusion, misinformation, and disinformation that too often characterize much of our public discourse. Instead, that loyalty, expressed as a reasoned faith in the promise of America as a self-correcting society, must of neces-

sity be contingent on rational thinking and the capacity of citizens to make informed decisions after they have weighed the proposals and counterproposals of contending factions and leaders. Only then can the oft-proclaimed social studies goal of effective citizenship education become more than a remote ideal.

References

Allen, Charles H., John Swett, and Josiah Royce. *Fourth Reader.* Indianapolis: Indiana School Book Co., 1889.

American History Illustrated (November-December 1988): 32–45.

Austin, Nancy. "Diary of Three Mile Island Incident: 3/28/79–4/4/79." *Social Education* (October 1979): 458–459.

Barzun, Jacques. "Mysteries of American History." *American Heritage* (December 1990): 50–57.

Batson, Amanda D. "Comprehension Strategies Employed by Master Teacher in Secondary Level Social Studies." Ph.D. diss., New Mexico State University, 1982.

Bodle, Walter. "The Black Soldier in World War I." *Social Education* (February 1985): 129–130.

Burns, Paul, Betty D. Roe, and Elinor P. Ross. *Teaching Reading in Today's Elementary Schools.* Dallas, Texas: Houghton Mifflin, 1982.

Camperell, Kay, and Roger S. Knight. "Reading Research and Social Studies." In *Handbook of Research on Social Studies Teaching and Learning*, edited by James Shaver. New York: Macmillan, 1990.

Crosby, Alfred W. *The Columbian Voyages, the Columbian Exchange and Their Historians.* Washington, D.C.: American Historical Association, 1987.

Devine, Thomas G. *Teaching Reading Comprehension: From Theory to Practice.* Boston: Allyn and Bacon, 1986.

—–—. *Teaching Reading in the Elementary School.* Boston: Allyn and Bacon, 1989.

—–—. *Teaching Study Skills.* Boston: Allyn and Bacon, 1981.

Early, Margaret. *Reading to Learn in Grades 5–12.* New York: Harcourt, Brace, Jovanovich, 1984.

Epperson, James F. "History Mysteries." *American Heritage* (April 1991): 10–12.

Flynt, Wayne. *Cracker Messiah: Governor Sydney J. Catts of Florida.* Baton Rouge: Louisiana State University Press, 1977.

Freeman, Elsie T., Walter Bodle, and Wynell Burroughs. "Eleanor Roosevelt Resigns from the DAR: A Study in Conscience." *Social Education* (November–December 1984): 536–541.

Gagnon, Paul. *Democracy's Half Told Story.* Washington, D.C.: American Federation of Teachers, 1989.

Goodman, Kenneth S. "Unity in Reading." In *Becoming*

Readers in a Complex Society, edited by Alan C. Purvis and Olive Niles. 83rd Yearbook of the National Society for the Study of Education. Chicago: University of Chicago Press, 1984.

Gunther, Deborah, Lynda Martin, Joan Maxwell, and Jeri Weiss. *Writing: A Sourcebook of Exercises.* Reading, Mass.: Addison-Wesley, 1978.

Hennings, Dorothy G. *Communication in Action: Teaching the Language Arts.* Boston: Houghton Mifflin, 1986.

"Hiroshima." *Tallahassee* [Florida] *Democrat,* August 6, 1986: 8.

Jennings, Francis. *The Invasion of America: Indians, Colonialism, and the Cant of Conquest.* Englewood Cliffs, N.J.: Prentice Hall, 1975.

Klein, Marvin L. *Teaching Reading Comprehension and Vocabulary.* Englewood Cliffs, N.J.: Prentice Hall, 1988.

Lash, Joseph. *Eleanor and Franklin.* New York: W.W. Norton and Co., 1971.

Lutz, William. "Fourteen Years of Doublespeak." *English Journal* (March 1988): 40–44.

Manchester, William. *American Caesar: Douglas MacArthur, 1880–1964.* Boston: Little, Brown, and Co., 1978.

Nichols, James N. "Using Prediction to Increase Content Area Interest and Understanding." *Journal of Reading* (December 1983): 225–233.

Phillips, Richard C. *Teaching for Thinking in High School Social Studies.* Reading, Mass.: Addison-Wesley, 1974.

Rank, Hugh. "Teaching About Public Persuasion: Rationale and Schema." In *Teaching About Doublespeak,* edited by Daniel Dieterich. Urbana, Ill.: National Council of Teachers of English, 1976.

Rissler, Herbert. "D. C. Stephenson and the Indiana Ku Klux Klan, 1920-25." *Indiana Social Studies Quarterly* (Spring 1966): 29–39.

Russell, David H. *Children's Thinking.* Waltham, Mass.: Blaisdel Publishers, 1956.

Sale, Kirkpatrick. *The Conquest of Paradise.* New York: Alfred A. Knopf, 1990.

Schiffers, Heinrich. *The Quest for Africa.* New York: G. P. Putnam's Sons, 1957.

Shofner, Jerl. *Nor Is It Over Yet: Florida in the Era of Reconstruction, 1853–1877.* Gainesville: University of Florida Press, 1974.

Smith, Bonnie. "Critically Reading for Propaganda Techniques." *Master's Thesis,* Rutgers University, 1974.

Smith, Carl B. "Two Approaches to Reading." *The Reading Teacher* (December 1990): 350–351.

Smith, Fredrick R., and Karen Feathers. "The Role of Reading in Content Classrooms: Assumption vs. Reality." *Journal of Reading* (December 1983): 266–282.

Splaine, John. "The Mass Media as an Influence on Social Studies." In *Handbook of Research on Social Studies Teaching and Learning,* edited by James Shaver. New York: Macmillan, 1990.

Stanley, Henry M. *Through the Dark Continent.* New York: Harper and Brothers, 1885.

Stanley, Julia P. "The Stylistics of Belief." In *Teaching About Doublespeak,* edited by Daniel Dietrich. Urbana, Ill.: National Council of Teachers of English, 1976.

Steele, Ronald D. "'Glory' Raises Many Questions." *The Washington* [D.C.] *Informer,* February 1–7, 1990: 8.

Stofner, Jeri. "Nor is it over yet." In *Florida in the Era of Reconstruction, 1853–1877.* Gainesville: University of Florida Press, 1974.

Thistlewaite, Linda L. "Critical Reading for At-Risk Students." *Journal of Reading* (May 1990): 586–593.

Wardell, Patricia M. "The Development and Evaluation of a Reading Program Designed to Improve Specific Skills in Reading Newspapers." Ph.D. diss., Boston University, 1973.

Chapter 4

Linking History, Literature, and Students

A primary reason for studying history is to furnish students with a microcosm beyond their own, away from the present, so that they can draw comparisons from it. Students strengthen their sense of identity as they determine how they resemble or differ from others. Through literature, students meet individuals from the past who were also timid, stubborn, energetic. Most importantly, students discover that they too belong in the chain of civilization, linked through history with people who felt, wondered, doubted, and dreamed as they do. As Ravitch and Finn emphasized:

> Facts are very important, but they must be used judiciously, so that students are able to understand what happened in the past and why they should learn about it. The basic facts of history are meaningless unless they illuminate a significant story. History should be taught in context, and emphasis should be placed on the significance of major events, people, trends, and turning points in the past. Without such context, students cannot understand the relations among events or derive from their study of history any truly important conceptual understanding. (1987, 205–206)

Classes in which extensive content coverage and factual recall direct the curriculum are not conducive environments for analysis, evaluation, and interpretation of historical evidence. Tomlinson, Tunnell, and Richgels (1993, 57) presented an argument for the use of trade books in social studies classrooms: "Writing in history textbooks is almost exclusively exposition, that is, presentation and explication of facts. Many recent research studies, however, suggest that narrative is a preferable form for presenting history to students." According to a study with sixth graders, instruction that provided time to build a substantive context for historical understanding through narratives resulted in greater interest and enthusiasm from students, who were then willing to investigate more traditional sources of information (Levstik 1986).

This chapter focuses on historical narratives, promising resources for linking students with the past, and then provides a rationale for using historical narratives in teaching history. Other subjects within the social studies may also be enhanced by the use of narrative literature and informational trade books, but the focus here remains on history. An instructional approach is suggested, followed by specific strategies to assist teachers in using historical narratives successfully in the classroom. The chapter ends with a list of selected historical literature arranged by historical eras.

Linking with the Past Through Historical Narratives

What, then, is the most formative way to induce historical understanding, to link students with their past? We begin with what students know best and expand upon it. Moffett (1968, 49) claimed that what children know best is story: "They utter themselves almost entirely through stories–real or invented–and they apprehend what others say through story. Children must represent in one mode of discourse–the narrative level of abstraction–several kinds of conceptions that in the adult world would be variously represented at several layers of abstraction." Through their reading, writing, and conversing, students become quite familiar with characters, events, and settings. Their constructs stem from a narrative framework.

Britton asserted, moreover, that:

[As] children read stories they enter into the experiences of other people. A child approaches the facts of history by involving himself in the lives of people of past ages, and the facts of geography by involving himself in the lives of people of other countries. It is through sharing their experiences that he moves towards an impersonal appreciation of historical and geographical issues. (1970, 154)

In historical fiction, "the human, everyday side of history is seen. Children understand that history was made by people like themselves" (Lynch-Brown and Tomlinson 1993). Children increase their abilities to understand history presented in narrative; as a result, interest in continuing the study of history is stimulated (Levstik 1983). The narrative format promotes historical learning through story structure, through concern with intention and action, through a strong sense of reality, through personal contact with history, through character identification, through the presentation of diverse perspectives, through humor, and through a blend of fantasy and reality. Each of these is explained more fully in the following sections.

Story Structure

According to Aristotle, the story has a beginning that elicits an expectation, a middle that often confounds, and an end that addresses the expectation. The implications of a single historical event cannot be fully understood simply because history is never-ending. When new episodes become history, we often revise our interpretations of the past. In particular, we reevaluate our feelings–whether an event was good or bad, and whether we are sorry or glad it happened. However, trapped within a story's structure, historical events become static, and their meaning can be interpreted without the threat of change. Each event finds its reserved spot within a whole context. A well-written narrative invites travel to a past world, a complex world of relationships, creating an integrated and integral pattern of human lives (Cianciolo 1981).

Intention and Action

Bruner (1986) suggested that narrative, like history, is concerned with intention and action, the consequences of both, and the particular: not just any person, but this person at this time and place, given this set of circumstances. Plot makes meaning possible and attracts attention to causation and motivation. The causes for events become explicit, and people's motivations become evident. Reality is sensed–not because events happened, but because they were remembered and fit coherently to illustrate a human story.

Power of Reality and Immediacy

Historical narrative possesses the power of reality itself. Narrative structures reality by imposing a predictable coherence that is traditional with stories. In this respect, historical narrative helps students find their community identities, bridging between present and past. By enlivening people from the past, narrative conveys ancestors as complex individuals who share many students' fears and failures, wishes and values (Pappas, Kiefer, and Levstik 1990). Narrative supports the need of students to interpret the human experience, to interact with others more effectively, and to gain meaningful knowledge. Thus, narratives help arouse historical interest, construct temporal and causal frameworks for historical understanding, and demonstrate the interpretive nature of history.

Students, by the nature of their age, frequent the present. Historical fiction author Erik Haugaard spoke about this here-and-now perspective that young people conveniently assume. He suggested that because they are absorbed in so many experiences each hour, children are not free to transcend the present. They tend to resist movement into a distant past or far future. Children categorize events before their birthdates as prehistory and consider them irrelevant (Cianciolo 1981). Through well-written and -researched works of historical fiction, students can identify with individuals of the past and come to know their problems, feelings, thoughts, life situations; this identification makes the journey into history easier.

Personal Contact with History

Providing more than an objective record of the past, historical fiction can guide students toward personal contact with history. It can kindle feelings for people who populated the past and influenced the present, fostering growth in historical imagination and understanding. By reconstructing the period in which a novel is set, students examine the everyday routines of people from the past: how they struggled, what they laughed and cried about, what they ate and wore, what they did for entertainment, which events and people influenced their thoughts and actions, and how their lives compare to present-day living. Without this ability to experience the past, students consider history a boring subject filled with dull wars and tedious dates.

Identification with Characters

Textbooks rarely spotlight the human dimension of historical events. But novels such as Pam Conrad's *Prairie Songs* (1985),

Kathryn Lasky's *Beyond the Divide* (1981), and Paul Fleischman's *The Borning Room* (1991) describe the daily lives of frontier families and permit readers to empathize with the characters portrayed. When the author is gifted, historical evidence requires no modification or falsification. In fact, one 10-year-old perceived the process of writing historical fiction as "taking the facts and wrapping paragraphs around them" (Levstik 1983, 234). In the company of ordinary people who step from historical fiction novels, students envision the past based on everyday experiences, desires unfulfilled, dreams realized, and frustrations felt.

In their efforts to fill fiction with rich and relevant historical content, an increasing number of authors are relying on the literary style of diaries or letters. Examples are Joan Blos's *A Gathering of Days: A New England Girl's Journal, 1830-1832* (1971), Patricia MacLachlan's *Sarah, Plain and Tall* (1985), and Brett Harvey's *Cassie's Journey: Going West in the 1860s* (1988) and *My Prairie Year: Based on the Diary of Elenore Plaisted* (1986). These literary devices divulge thoughts and feelings previously private or unknown and confirm that people respond in similar and diverse, expected and unexpected ways. When students identify with characters from historical fiction and respond as the characters do, their imaginations are activated.

Diverse Perspectives

Usually, historical fiction describes personal decisions tied to past events. Such literature can function as a springboard for examining diverse perspectives, for distinguishing facts from opinions, and for understanding the difficulties of resolving conflict. As students read and discuss, they begin to understand the distinct ways in which facts and interpretations paint a historical backdrop. For example, students might search the following books for different facets of slavery: James Lincoln Collier and Christopher Collier's *Jump Ship to Freedom* (1981) and *War Comes to Willy Freeman* (1983); Patricia Beatty's *Jayhawker* (1991); Belinda Hurmence's *A Girl Called Boy* (1982); and Paula Fox's *The Slave Dancer* (1973).

Humor

Another advantage of this genre in contrast to the history text lies in the author's freedom to inject historical events and personalities with a touch of humor. Textbook writers feel compelled to present their topics seriously, whereas historical fiction writers can entertain with comic relief. Examples of historical narratives that weave humor into the story are: Sid Fleischman's *Mr. Mysterious & Company* (1962) and his *Humbug Mountain* (1978); Patricia Gauch's *This Time, Tempe Wick?* (1974); Elizabeth George Speare's *The Sign of the Beaver* (1983); Jean Fritz's *Will You Sign Here, John Hancock?* (1976); F. N. Monjo's *King George's Head Was Made of Lead* (1974); and Betty Bao Lord's *In the Year of the Boar and Jackie Robinson* (1984). Robert Lawson in *Ben and Me* and *Mr. Revere and I* took an unusual approach to his biographical fantasies of famous American political figures by telling their stories humorously through the eyes of an animal.

Fantasy and Reality Interwoven

Some historical novels clearly link past and present; others suggest a vague connection that can be clarified through discussion. One literary genre that seems to be gaining in popularity is a mixture of historical fiction and modern fantasy. Usually called historical fantasy, stories from this sub-genre begin in the present and provide the exposition of characters and conflict within a modern-day time frame. After the exposition, the main character moves through time into the past. This time shift permits the main character to react to the past in much the same way a student might view the past; meanwhile, the characters who inhabit only the past era present their

world and its customs as they were. The present-day character finds the past world strange in ways similar to what students find. Examples of good historical fantasies for students are Janet Lunn's *The Root Cellar* (1983), Jean Marzollo's *Halfway Down Paddy Lane* (1981), Kevin Major's *Blood Red Ochre* (1989), Belinda Hurmence's *A Girl Called Boy* (1982), and Pam Conrad's *Stonewords: A Ghost Story* (1990). Because of more complex plot development, most time-shift stories seem especially appropriate for students in fifth grade and above.

Uses of Historical Narratives in the Social Studies Curriculum

Historical fiction can function in a number of capacities: as a key to historical data, as supplemental reading, as a resource for further study, as an introduction to an era, as background material for the teacher, as literature for independent reading, and as motivation for students not interested in textbook history. Most importantly, historical fiction features the human contributions to historical events, humanizing history and sowing seeds that sprout historical understanding (Freeman and Levstik 1988).

Caution is necessary, however, because students are not naturally critical of historical narratives. They might formulate misconceptions about historical events, personalities, and eras. Students may overgeneralize when exposed to a single account or viewpoint. Teachers need to be aware of these limitations and know how to compensate for them. Instructional techniques are crucial. For historical fiction to be an effective resource, teachers must incorporate critical analysis into instruction. Adept teachers elicit questions that challenge published "truths." They expect their students to investigate multiple sources for information, to look for how historical interpretations compare with each other. When characters are fictitious and events fabricated, teachers can involve students in distinguishing fact from fiction. They can help students identify stereo-types and determine whether these stereotypes accurately depict period attitudes and beliefs rather than author bias. Critical thinking is sharpened as students recognize the author's point of view, possible bias, and opposing in-terpretations of fact (Freeman and Levstik 1988). Historical fiction, then, holds the power to transport students from an ethnocentric, fragmented world into a complex, interdependent one. It affords them opportunities to participate and to develop the framework req-uisite for sorting and interpreting the daily deluge of information (National Council for the Social Studies 1989).

Discussion of historical fiction in a social studies class could include the following questions:

1. What research formed the basis of the novel? (Check prologue, epilogue, endnotes, bibliography, or other statements by the author.)
2. Can the historical details be verified? What sources might provide corroboration?
3. Which details of setting does the author present to readers? Do these details lend authenticity to the story?
4. What interpretation of history does the story present?
5. What viewpoints are presented through the characters' actions and words?
6. Which parts (characters, events, places) of the novel are fictitious or exaggerated? How do you know or why do you think so?
7. What interesting historical information did you learn from this book that you had not acquired through the textbook?
8. Compare the events from several histori-cal fiction books from the same era. How do they corroborate one another? In what ways do they diverge?
9. Compare the events as portrayed in the novels with the events as presented in the textbook.
10. After reading the events from a textbook, describe how you feel about the events.

How do you feel after reading about the same events as presented in the novel?

Sometimes historical fiction for middle level and high school students concentrates on episodes of inhumanity: Nazi atrocities, injustices showered upon American Indians or Japanese Americans, enslavement of Af-rican Americans in the United States for more than two centuries, devastation in-flicted by the atom bomb. Historical fiction also celebrates survivors. Many of these sto-ries are told by children who emerge with refreshing hopefulness and enthusiasm for life. Other historical novels have the power to evoke an aura of horrific fantasy that startles any student. The student begins to connect the story with the facts of history, evaluating both the events of history and the fictional story. The horror becomes real, the reality becomes surreal. Through this win-dow to a surreal past, the student—as a pro-tected observer, safe from the awful events being narrated—witnesses instances of humanity's capacity for inhumanity.

Social studies teachers hope that students will feel, as well as know, history. This is the legacy historical fiction can bestow: linking history and literature, calling to students who are eager to listen and to interpret; to meet characters who belong to earlier eras; to re-member events that presented choices, and choices that affected lives; to understand the people whose lives paved the way to the present; to travel the continuum that the past initiates; to reflect on the times that bind us together; and to be embraced by the human-ity of history.

Strategies for Linking Literature and History

In this section, strategies for humanizing history are presented. The challenge is to mix and match, modify and manipulate these sug-gestions. Teachers can tailor the strategies to the interests and abilities of different students. Students can offer their insights and innova-tions also. The interpretive nature of history can be demonstrated through questioning. As instruction moves farther from the textbook, and students move further into historical literature, the deeper and more permanent their historical understandings will become. Students will not just browse through historical information; they will imagine, feel, and remember history.

In this section of the chapter, we propose strategies for involving students with historical literature: by capturing their interest and captivating their minds with literary selections, by integrating and improving the role of reading and writing in the history classroom, and by supplementing the history text with the human side of past events. Several how-to guides for planning, modeling, and initiating a history program include reading aloud to your students, providing them time for silent reading, using literature response groups, establishing dialogue journals, introducing student learning logs, and guiding student simulations.

Reading Aloud to Your Students

Literature offers educational bonuses, in addition to providing entertainment. For this reason, sharing literature with students should be much more prevalent than it is. One of the best ways to share literature is by reading aloud, which, as students move to middle school and high school levels, is unfortunately no longer a routine practice (Huck, Hepler, and Hickman 1993). Yet reading literature aloud can prove to be instrumental in boosting historical interest and understanding.

Consider the following criteria when selecting literature to share with a class:

- Find a story with a setting in the historical era under study that appears generally appropriate to students' developmental levels, literary backgrounds, and interests. You can judge this when you pre-read the book.
- Avoid reading aloud books that students will consume eagerly on their own. Let them

have the satisfaction of reading those books independently.
- Choose quality literature that will exercise imaginations, extend interests, and demonstrate fine writing and illustrating.
- Select a book that is personally pleasing and read it to yourself before reading it aloud (Huck, Hepler, and Hickman 1993).

Reading aloud presents opportunities for in-depth discussion of concepts merely suggested in a unit of study. A carefully selected work of historical fiction can serve as a schema or interest builder before students tackle the textbook. Or historical fiction can elaborate content during and after the reading of textual information. How are facts or events from the unit of study depicted in historical literature? By addressing questions that indicate subtle connections between textbook and historical fiction, students can amplify and deepen their understanding of historical concepts and content (Lynch-Brown 1990).

Following the read-aloud experience, response is the key element in effecting student entrance into the past via literature; oral and written response options are explained later in this chapter. Students need to be exposed to a broad spectrum of response types, then allowed the freedom to choose from several different response options. During a class period that is already over too quickly, some teachers hesitate to devote the time needed for reading aloud a full-length novel. The old bugaboo of coverage hangs heavy over the teacher! Some sensible solutions to this problem are possible. By reading aloud the exposition of the story, generally the first two or three chapters, and summarizing the main events leading to the climax, the book's climax and concluding chapters can then be read aloud, shortening the read-aloud time. Excerpting a book in this manner requires careful reading and reflecting on the part of the teacher beforehand to ensure a coherent story. Another strategy involves selecting a short story or picture book to share in one or two sittings. Teachers who acquire class sets of a historical novel may wish to read aloud the opening chapters of the book, then ask students to read the remainder of the novel to themselves.

Some read-aloud techniques proposed by Lynch-Brown follow:

Step 1. Select a book appropriate to the topic. Be sure the book has well-described characters to whom students can relate, a fairly fast-moving plot, and strong emotional appeal. Read the book to yourself before reading it aloud. You may encounter words that you need to practice for pronunciation and certain phrasings that need rehearsing. You will also want to know generally what to expect as you read the story aloud. Some books contain sensitive material you will want to consider how to treat.

Step 2. Minimize distractions by asking students to put papers, books, and pens aside and to remain quiet and seated. Be sure students are comfortable and relaxed. External distractions might be diminished by posting a sign on the door announcing read-aloud time.

Step 3. Give a brief introduction to the book before beginning to read aloud. Include the title, author, and some hint at the topic of the story in order to capture attention and build interest. It often helps if students determine how the story may relate to their lives or connect with their prior knowledge. For example, a teacher might say, "I will be reading the book *The Fire in the Stone* by Colin Thiele for the next few weeks. This story is set in Australia and is about a 14-year-old boy who makes friends with a boy of a different race. What do you know about Australia? What do you think the title refers to? Now let's see what happens in this

book." If the book has an illustrated cover, the teacher may also ask students to tell what they anticipate about the story based on the cover.

Step 4. Read fluently with lots of expression in your voice. Your voice is an effective tool for conveying the meaning, feeling, and drama of the story. You can vary your voice by using a low to high pitch, a soft to loud volume, and slow to fast pace. I usually begin a story with a soft, steady voice which permits me to change volume, pace, and pitch for the desired effect. Be dramatic!

Step 5. Maintain eye contact with the class while reading aloud. In this way, students feel closer to you and to the story.

Step 6. Break at a natural stopping point and elicit student reactions. It is neither necessary nor desirable to ask comprehension questions. (1990, 63)

Teachers can help students over the most difficult part of a chapter book, generally the exposition of the story that occurs in the first two or three chapters, by noting student confusion or waning interest, and interjecting some explanation as needed. Once the students are acquainted with the characters and understand the nature of the conflict in the story, they become hooked and want to hear the rest of the story as soon as possible.

Silent, Independent Reading

Until the 1950s, many students read regularly at home. They practiced reading skills naturally through their recreational reading. But with the debut of television as an accessible mode of entertainment, the number of students engaging in recreational reading has dropped substantially. Because reading is a less frequent habit established at home, teachers must set aside time for silent reading in the classroom. Since reading practice breeds student competence, class time for silent, independent reading is essential.

Teachers can assign independent reading

of historical narratives to students. Student cooperation can be enhanced by starting the silent reading in class. During this class period, students have an opportunity to get hooked on the books, increasing the likelihood that they will finish the books at home. Many schools have instituted sustained silent reading (SSR) programs to cultivate the habit of reading for enjoyment, but a sustained silent reading program can be modified so that it can also augment historical understanding.

In history class, SSR is a block of class time (15–30 minutes) reserved for perusal of material selected by students and teacher. In this situation, the material is selected from a unit reading list. The teacher models her role as an avid reader who enjoys historical literature, and the students are guaranteed uninterrupted time to explore their selections from the list (no chores attached; no related assignments, such as homework or reports). A book brigade emerges as students are surrounded by a teacher and peers involved with literature. They discover that reading can be fun and infectious. During SSR, this community of readers profits from time to investigate a world of historical narratives that supplement and enhance the history text. Teacher read-aloud, in-class sustained silent reading, and assigned out-of-class independent reading can provide students with the literary texts needed to arouse their historical imaginations.

Students may be expected to bring self-selected SSR materials to class. These materials, suggested in the social studies unit reading list, can be unit-related books or magazines. For students who arrive without materials or who finish their selections, a classroom table or shelf may be stocked with an adequate supply of inviting titles. SSR is not a privilege earned by the student who demonstrates acceptable behavior or completes assignments. Instead, it is a valued and enjoyed routine for all. As guest

readers, visitors can join the group and share their reading preferences. The principal, coaches, guidance counselors, and community members are guest-list possibilities.

Providing a few minutes for readers to respond orally or in writing to their selections stimulates thinking, enhances oral and written expressive language abilities, broadens perspectives, and promotes further reading. Dialogue journals, learning logs, and literature response groups are response channels that a flexible teacher can open to foster student involvement and interest. Teachers with assistance from the school media librarian also act as guides for locating literature that will intrigue their students.

Guidelines for Implementing SSR in a U.S. History Class

Step 1. Plan thematic units of study for each month or grading period on the school calendar. Examples of six six-week themes follow; recommended books for each of these eras can be found at the end of this chapter. Additional favorites can be added to these lists.

a) Prehistory/Exploration and Colonization of North America/Early American Frontier.
b) French and Indian War/American Revolution.
c) Industrial Revolution/War of 1812/American Indian/Western Frontier.
d) Slavery/Civil War/Post-Civil War/Immigration/Western Territories.
e) World War I/Prohibition/Great Depression.
f) World War II/Post-World War II/Civil Rights Era/Vietnam War.

Step 2. Locate the unit reading list that corresponds to the era planned for study and add your own favorites to the list. Browse through this list before introducing the era. Become familiar with as many titles as possible; stock the classroom library with material on the unit reading list. Involve your students by:

• Providing each student with a copy of the unit reading list.

- Explaining SSR–its purposes, as well as the purpose of the reading list.
- Encouraging students to search for unit-related reading material, contributing their finds to a temporary class collection.

Step 3. Distribute copies of the unit reading list to school and public librarians, as well as to local bookstores that cater to students.

Step 4. Daily, if possible, devote a few minutes to historical book talks, messages intended to hook students on quality works of historical fiction. The teacher can model these book commercials, then ask students to volunteer to present them. Whoever delivers the talk should have the book in hand and briefly touch on setting, main character, conflict, and several reasons for liking the story. Five or six sentences should suffice. A book talk might sound like this: "While reading Betty Baker's *A Stranger and Afraid* (1972), I could imagine how Sopete must have felt after he and his younger brother Zabe were kidnapped during a Pueblo Indian raid on his village. I understand why Sopete wanted Zabe to remember their Wichita language and past, and why he was so determined to run away–back to their father and familiar tribal customs. I am still thinking about Coronado and the Spaniards' quest for gold, the consequences of their march through Indian territory in the 1540s. These consequences changed Sopete's life as he found himself endangered by a friend's lie and back home without his brother. I liked this story because I came to know Sopete: his mind and spirit, his values and desires, his struggles and compromises."

Step 5. Post annotations of books from the unit reading list as a student reference or guide to help students determine their own book selections.

Step 6. After every SSR session, allow students five to fifteen minutes for response–in dialogue journals, learning logs, small literature response groups, or whole class discussions. Sharing responses prompts students to clarify and organize their thoughts and feelings. While listening to others, they open their perceptions to challenges and possible revision. This exercise usually triggers interest, leading to provocative questions and important discoveries about history.

Step 7. Implement SSR regularly and frequently. Using SSR once a month or twice a year will not have the effects nor yield the benefits that weekly or twice weekly SSR can promise. If lack of time is a real constraint, omit part of the existing program and substitute it with SSR for an adequate trial period.

The inclusion of SSR in a social studies class can readily be expanded into thematic history units that center on children's trade books. Downs (1993) describes how she plans and implements thematic history units throughout an entire school year in her class.

Eliciting Student Responses

The next part of the section on strategies proposes ways teachers can elicit students' oral and written responses to historical literature. Recommendations for student activities that cultivate historical imagination and understanding follow. As students share responses to literature with the teacher and with their classmates, they can develop critical thinking skills and fresh perspectives. They enjoy opportunities to relate and reshape personal constructs. Above all, the interpretive nature of history is realized as students themselves speculate and contemplate others' interpretations.

Literature Response Groups. Literature response groups provide students with opportunities to talk about books they have read. In the history classroom, these groups meet on specified dates to share reactions and relate their readings to the study unit. Initially, the teacher should determine group membership. Group size may vary. The teacher can assign more mature and peer-cooperative students to fewer and larger groups, with as many as seven members; less mature students seem to work best in groups of three or four. As students grow more accustomed to literature response meetings, they improve their abilities to function in groups (Lynch-Brown 1990).

The teacher can establish literature response groups in a variety of ways:

- Group together readers of the same book or author.
- Group together readers of books with similar themes.
- Group together readers of books that depict similar settings or historical events.
- Group together readers of different genres of books. For example, students reading historical fiction and a student reading nonfiction on a similar topic can benefit by assignment to the same group.
- Group together readers of books with similar historical settings, but with different characters or viewpoints.

Student membership in groups often changes after they have discussed completed books and have opened new books.

Literature response groups engage in highly structured or open-ended activities. A combination of both seems to be most successful. Each student in a response group introduces her or his book with a book talk. First, the student shows the book to the other group members. Having the book in hand is essential for attracting students' attention to the book. The book talk starts with reference to author and title, then concludes with five to eight sentences summarizing the story and expressing personal reactions. This type of report avoids revealing resolutions or climaxes. After a book talk, other students in the group are encouraged to ask questions, offer their responses to the reviewed book, or compare the facts from the novel to the textbook information being studied. The book is usually circulated for closer perusal by individuals. Figure 4.1 provides a sample chart that groups of students can use to compare information from textbooks and trade books. Before literature response groups meet, the teacher might reproduce this chart to aid discussion during or after book talks (Lynch-Brown 1990, 164).

Dialogue Journals. One reliable predictor of student involvement is personal response: when students link stories about others' lives to their own experiences, and when they share the same beliefs and emotions as characters in a book. Written response to literature compels reflection and refines interpretation. It also provides a forum for peer idea exchanges and yields strategies for sustaining written discourse and developing skill in critical think-

Figure 4.1
Comparing Information in Textbooks and Trade Books

Traits	Textbooks	Trade Books
Social		
Economic		
Political		
Historical		
Geographic		

ing. Because response in a dialogue journal stems from individual interest, the motivation to discover new information is self-initiating and fulfilling (Atwell 1987).

Essentially, the dialogue journal furnishes a medium for the written interchange of ideas between two people—teacher and student, or student and peer. It grows into a record of correspondence between individuals who wish to compare how each thinks and feels. Exposing never-before-considered perspectives and a forum for inquiry, the dialogue journal expedites clarity and expansion of thought. The teacher models response by sharing personal insights and posing provocative questions, one per journal entry. Influenced by teacher demonstrations, student correspondents write what is important to them. Soon, students can open the channels of thinking and feeling through written dialogues they coordinate among themselves and with their teacher. As Atwell explained:

> There is no one set of questions to ask every reader; there are, instead, individual readers with their own strategies, questions, tastes, and styles. There is no one correct way to approach or interpret a text; there are, instead, individual readers with an incredible range of prior knowledge and experience. Through the dialogue journals I've discovered alternative ways a junior high . . . teacher can talk to students about literature. The letters I write to readers are personal and contextual. That is, what I say in my half of the dialogue journal comes from my knowledge of how the student reads and thinks, of what the student knows. Response grows both from what I've learned about a reader and how I hope to move the reader's thinking. (1987, 178)

General principles for teachers to apply as they respond in dialogue journals follow:
- Respond specifically and honestly, but not too personally. Support your statements with reasons, examples, and experience. Dialogue journals hinge on academic subjects under scrutiny in the classroom. Their purpose is to determine what information the writer would like to know more about, not to unload private problems or provide counsel.
- Dialogue journal writing is first-draft material, not polished final copy. As such, teachers should not evaluate it for errors. The focus is communication of ideas. Read dialogue journals for meaning, not for mistakes.
- Dialogue journals are not intended to test reading comprehension. In responding, refrain from smothering students with questions. One thought-provoking question is sufficient.
- Push students into the literature for critical evaluation and analysis, encouraging them to dig deeper than summation of plot requires. Challenge them to speculate on the human aspects: the motivations and intentions hidden in character conversations, actions, and reactions.
- Learn about your students through the written dialogue; use this knowledge to extend their knowledge. With student permission, read aloud significant entries so that the whole class can learn from them.

Learning Logs. To transfer responsibility for learning to students and to stimulate thinking through writing, the teacher can introduce learning logs to his or her class. A learning log is a variation on dialogue journals that facilitates thinking and writing across the curriculum. According to Pappas, Kiefer, and Levstik (1990, 291), students use these logs to "plan, map, record, recall, consider, organize, assign, remember, pose, question, predict, decide, and so on," while involved in a variety of study unit activities. Thinking on paper promotes student awareness and control of the learning process, providing students with necessary practice as reflective, productive learners.

Learning logs supply the occasion for contemplation. Associated with writing in learning logs are three interdependent processes: asking questions, formulating guesses or stating hypotheses, and organizing ideas (Pappas, Kiefer, and Levstik 1990, 291). Explanations of each process in relation to the learning log follow:

- *Asking questions.* Traditionally, students do not ask questions but they expect to answer questions from others. Learning logs furnish the context for students to become the inquirers. Students use the logs to list their questions before, during, and after reading or discussion. Their inquiries serve several purposes: to initiate small group interaction; to document what students hope to discover about a particular unit of study; to remind students during the planning stage of a project or presentation; and to extend contemplation at the conclusion of a project or activity.

- *Formulating hypotheses.* If it is crucial for students to inquire, it is just as vital that they build hypotheses while answering their own and others' questions. As Pappas, Kiefer, and Levstik explained:

  Learning logs can help children to make educated guesses. They look for clues and connections as they read, hear their peers' ideas . . . engage in an experiment; they revise and reconsider as they examine others' feedback, read another book on the same topic, see a teacher demonstration; they predict, propose, and confirm in their own reading, in a class discussion or presentation, in deciding what and how to write. (1990, 291)

- *Organizing ideas.* If learning hinges upon reconstruction of knowledge, then teachers must encourage students to probe for patterns and connections. Learning logs assist students during active organization of their ideas by recording patterns and calling attention to connections. Categorizing

questions and hypotheses can facilitate reading, writing, and understanding in general. As a preface to study, mapping out a topic can stimulate peer interaction, encourage student scrutiny, and establish the basis for drafting and revising.

Student-centered learning logs document content and thinking processes. They constitute a convenient vehicle product for teacher observation and offer an instrument for student reflection. Usually, the learning log is a spiral-bound notebook or a three-ring binder. A separate section might be designated for each unit of study. The student dates all entries in the log. Most teachers respond in logs with comments on content; they request clarification or pose questions students should consider.

For students who have no experience with learning logs, teachers might introduce the concept through a mini-lesson. They can refer to the categories of asking questions, formulating hypotheses, and organizing ideas as ways to structure entries. Learning logs are stored in a classroom location conveniently accessible to teacher and students. The teacher reviews and responds to the logs daily or weekly; students can recover them at the start of each day (Pappas, Kiefer, and Levstik 1990).

By using learning logs in the history classroom, students can register comparisons between textbook and trade books. The logs can provide a place for charting conflicting or confirming interpretations. If a student requires additional source material for purposes of verification, the learning log can function as a detective's notebook to be filled with questions, hypotheses, and investigative results. A record of speculations and supporting details, the learning log can deepen historical understanding and offer evidence of history's interpretive nature. In addition, teachers can expect students to describe in their logs the human side of history. They can focus on a fact or event of interest mentioned in the history textbook, and then draw on historical fiction and their imaginations to develop a humanistic context. Documenting responses in learning logs or dialogue journals supplies pages of possibilities worth sharing.

Simulations. Historical fiction (as well as primary and secondary source material) abounds with situations ripe for simulation—e.g., dramatizing historical events, conversations, or confrontations. Simulations can be performed with improvised dialogue and little or nothing in the way of props, costumes, and stage settings. Because literature provides the contextual substance, students can more readily assume roles performed by past personalities. The literature has delineated circumstances for students; it has drawn a detailed historical atmosphere. And the literature has conveyed hints of appropriate-for-the-times behavior, beliefs, and motives through characters' thoughts, actions, and words. Reserved for the student or student groups are decisions based on their interpretations:

- Had I been in that place at that time under those circumstances, what might I have said?
- What might I have done?
- Shedding my 1990s perspective, what choices might be open to me? Which would I think the best, and why?
- What might be the consequences of each choice?
- How might my life be different from or the same as it is today?
- Considering a set of characters bound by a given historical event or era, which character's role would I want to assume, and why?

If a group of students has shared and enjoyed a work of historical fiction, that group may want to simulate a favorite conflict or event from the story. Supplementing or verifying the historical event with primary or secondary sources can be instrumental in developing a believable simulation. Working co-operatively in small groups, the students should discuss, rehearse, and then complete the simulation. The teacher guides by helping each group design an initial framework for their simulations. They might choose to focus on one of several aspects: the primary historical event or chain of events; the major conflict and its resolution or an alternate resolution determined by group consensus; or the characters from history, their reactions, and interactions.

After students have prepared and rehearsed dramatic simulations, they should share their simulations with the entire class. Discussion can follow and may provoke more careful consideration of historical issues raised during the presentations. Dramas from the past reenacted by student troupes are thus burned into memories through active and imaginative participation.

Other Book-Related Activities. Following are additional suggestions for using trade books in class.

- Prepare a brief biography of the author and present it orally or in writing.
- Develop a television script based on one exciting scene from the book. Groups could select, plan, write, and present different scenes.
- Describe the setting of the book and explain how the setting was important to the events.
- Select one character from the book to describe in detail: physical appearance; emotional, mental, and physical attributes; kinds of friends and family; and other characteristics.
- Tell what kind of reader would enjoy the book and why.
- Discuss why you think the author wrote the book and what you believe the author hoped readers would get from the book.
- Write a first-person description of an event in the story, told as though the writer were an onlooker.

- In a group, plan and write a sequel to the story. Compare sequels written by different groups.
- Develop a list of new words and their meanings. Explore foreign words and phrases.
- Compare the facts found in the trade book with those found in the textbook. Look for agreement and contradictions. Seek additional sources to determine authenticity. Write to the author, requesting information about sources that provided an historical framework for the book (Lynch-Brown 1990, 167).

In the history classroom, students can use oral and written discourse to synthesize information from the textbook and historical narratives. Too often, textbooks omit traces of human forces from a textbook's factual representation of the past. Response to historical fiction, however, uncovers the humanistic perspective for consideration against the backdrop of the history text. Brozo and Tomlinson (1986) suggested several simple yet worthwhile activities that permit students to interpret and personalize newly acquired knowledge, while allowing teachers to check for student learning and possible misconceptions. Students can incorporate their activities in a variety of journal entries:

- on-the-scene descriptions of places or events merely noted in the text but detailed in a work of historical fiction;
- letters to historical figures from students who imaginatively slip into the skins of fictional characters;
- discourse between historical figures and fictional characters;
- creation of an informative picture storybook by modeling a plot from historical fiction and including facts from the history text;
- writing a newspaper article (the class can combine articles for their own paper from the past).

Social studies teachers who experiment with historical fiction in their classes will uncover many more student activities and projects related to outstanding works of historical literature. The rewards for teachers can be in watching students who enjoy history as never before and who read with greater interest, ease, and fluency than ever.

Selected Narrative Literature by U.S. Historical Eras

The books listed in the following bibliography are highlighted for their literary merit and potential for nurturing historical understanding and imagination. Books have been grouped into six eras of U.S. history and briefly annotated for interest levels, locales, and dates of settings. Some books set in other countries, but on topics typically treated in U.S. history courses, are also included. For example, books dealing with the Holocaust in Germany are listed so that students will be provided a fuller context for that period of U.S. history. Following this list are some sources to locate narrative literature to incorporate into world history units.

Many of the titles on the following list make excellent read-aloud books. Any book a teacher plans to read aloud should be read first by the teacher. When previewing a book, consider difficult pronunciations, sensitive wordings or values and students' need for prior knowledge.

All titles are suitable for independent reading by students; some of the books on this recommended list have a lighter, humorous tone and are included in order to appeal to different types of readers. All listed books can provide history students and teachers with worthwhile background information, historical ambience, and a humanistic context for historic facts and figures. *(Ages refer to approximate interest levels. YA = young adult readers.)*

Prehistory/Exploration and Colonization of North America/Early American Frontier (up to 1685)
Baker, Betty. *The Blood of the Brave.* New York: Harper, 1966. Ages 11-YA. Spanish exploration of the New World, early 1500s.
------. *A Stranger and Afraid.* New York: Macmillan, 1972. Ages 11-YA. Native

American tribes, 1540s.

—. *Walk the World's Rim.* New York: Harper, 1965. Ages 11-YA. Spanish explorers sail from Cuba, land in Florida, then to Mexico, 1520s.

Baumann, Hans. *Son of Columbus.* New York: Oxford, 1957. Ages 11-YA. Spanish exploration of the New World, early 1500s.

Beatty, John and Patricia. *Campion Towers.* New York: Macmillan, 1965. Ages 12-YA. U.S., Salem colony, England, 1650s.

—. *Pirate Royal.* New York: Macmillan, 1969. Ages 12-YA. English protagonist is deported to Massachusetts Bay Colony, but becomes a pirate of Spanish ships, 1660s.

Bowen, Gary. *Stranded at Plimoth Plantation 1626.* Illustrated by Gary Bowen. New York: HarperCollins, 1994. Jamestown, settler life, 1620s.

Brenner, Barbara. *If You Were There in 1492.* New York: Bradbury, 1991. Ages 10-14. This nonfiction work takes a trip back in time to present the culture and civilization of Europe at this time.

Clapp, Patricia. *Constance: A Story of Early Plymouth.* New York: Lothrop, 1968. Ages 10-14. U.S. colonial era, 1620s.

Dorris, Michael. *Morning Girl.* New York: Hyperion, 1992. Ages 9-12. Taino Indians, Bahamian island, 1492.

Fleischman, Paul. *Saturnalia.* New York: Harper, 1990. Ages 12-YA. Boston, Narraganset Indians, 1680s.

Fritz, Jean, Katherine Paterson, Patricia and Frederick McKissack, Margaret Mahy, and Jamake Highwater. *The World in 1492.* Illustrated by Stefano Vitale. New York: Holt, 1992. Ages 9-YA. A nonfiction work with interesting chapters on Europe, Asia, Australia and Oceania, and the Americas portrays the lives of many of the peoples of that time period.

Kohler, Jackie French. *The Primrose.* San Diego: Harcourt, 1992. Ages 13-YA. Love story with an English girl and a Native American boy, Puritan Colony in Massa-

chusetts, 1600s.

O'Dell, Scott. *The Captive.* New York: Houghton, 1979. Ages 12-YA. First of trilogy which includes *The Feathered Serpent,* Houghton, 1981; and *The Amethyst Ring,* Houghton, 1983. Spanish exploration of the New World (Mexico), early to mid-1500s.

—. *The King's Fifth.* New York: Houghton, 1966. Ages 11-YA. Spanish exploration of the New World, 1540s.

Pelta, Kathy. *Discovering Christopher Columbus: How History Is Invented.* Minneapolis, MN: Lerner, 1991. Ages 9-YA. A biography of Columbus with an emphasis on how historians research the truth about his life.

Roop, Peter and Connie. *I, Columbus: My Journal 1492-3.* Illustrated by Peter E. Hanson. New York: Walker, 1990. Ages 9-14. In this nonfiction work a prologue and an epilogue tie together passages from Columbus's ship journal for interesting insights into his journey.

Steele, William O. *The Magic Amulet.* San Diego: Harcourt, 1979. Ages 10-14. North America, 10,000 B.C.

Treece, Henry. *Westward to Vinland.* Chatham, NY: Phillips, 1967. Ages 11-14. Vikings to North America, 960-1013.

Yolen, Jane. *Encounter.* Illustrated by David Shannon. San Diego: Harcourt, 1992. Ages 7-12. A picture book that tells the story of a Taino Indian boy who witnesses the landing of Columbus and his men on the island of San Salvador.

French and Indian War/American Revolution (1685-1785)

Avi. *The Fighting Ground.* Philadelphia, PA: Lippincott, 1984. Ages 10-14. U.S. Revolutionary War era, 1770s.

—. *Night Journeys.* New York: Pantheon, 1979. Ages 8-11. U.S. colonial era, 1770s.

Caudill, Rebecca. *The Far-off Land.* New York: Viking, 1964. Ages 11-14. U.S. frontier, 1780s.

Clapp, Patricia. *I'm Deborah Sampson: A Sol-*

dier in the War of the Revolution. New York: Lothrop, 1977. Ages 9-12. U.S., 1770s.

—. *Witches' Children: A Story of Salem.* New York: Lothrop, 1982. Ages 10-YA. U.S. colonial era, 1690s.

Collier, James Lincoln, and Christopher Collier. *Jump Ship to Freedom.* New York: Delacorte, 1981. Ages 9-12. U.S., slavery, 1780s.

—. *My Brother Sam Is Dead.* New York: Four Winds, 1974. Ages 10-14. U.S. Revolutionary War era, 1770s.

—. *War Comes to Willy Freeman.* New York: Delacorte, 1983. Ages 9-12. U.S., African-Americans, 1780s.

Forbes, Esther. *Johnny Tremain.* New York: Houghton, 1943. Ages 10-13. U.S. Revolutionary War era, 1770s.

Fritz, Jean. *The Cabin Faced West.* New York: Coward, 1958. Ages 7-10. U.S. pioneers, 1700s.

—. *Will You Sign Here, John Hancock?* New York: Coward, 1976. Ages 7-10. U.S. Declaration of Independence, humorous biography.

Gauch, Patricia. *This Time, Tempe Wick?* New York: Coward, 1974. Ages 7-10. U.S. Revolutionary War era, 1780s.

Lasky, Kathryn. *Beyond the Burning Time.* New York: Scholastic, 1994. Ages 11-14. Salem witch trials, 1690s.

Lawson, Robert. *Ben and Me.* Boston: Little, 1939. Ages 9-12. Ben Franklin's life told through the eyes of his mouse. U.S., 1700s.

—. *Mr. Revere and I.* Boston: Little, 1953. Ages 10-14. U.S. Revolutionary War era, Revere's ride told from point of view of his horse.

Monjo, F.N. *King George's Head Was Made of Lead.* New York: Coward, 1974. Ages 7-10. U.S. Revolutionary War era, New York.

O'Dell, Scott. *Sarah Bishop.* New York: Houghton, 1980. Ages 10-14. U.S. Revolutionary War era, 1770s.

Petry, Ann. *Tituba of Salem Village.* New York: Crowell, 1964. Ages 10-14. U.S. colonial era, 1690s.

Rinaldi, Ann. *A Break with Charity: A Story About the Salem Witch Trials.* San Diego: Gulliver, 1992. Ages 13-YA. Witch trials, Massachusetts, 1692.

—. *The Fifth of March: A Story of the Boston Massacre.* San Diego: Harcourt, 1993. Ages 11-14. Indentured servitude in Boston, 1770s.

Speare, Elizabeth George. *The Sign of the Beaver.* New York: Houghton, 1983. Ages 8-12. Maine frontier, 1700s.

—. *The Witch of Blackbird Pond.* New York: Houghton, 1958. Ages 10-14. U.S. colonial era, late 1680s.

Industrial Revolution/War of 1812/American Indians/Western Frontier (1785-1830s)

Avi. *The True Confessions of Charlotte Doyle.* New York: Orchard, 1990. Ages 8-12. England, United States, 1830s.

Beatty, Patricia. *Who Comes with Cannons?* New York: Morrow, 1992. Ages 9-12. North Carolina, Underground Railroad.

Berry, James. *Ajeemah and His Son.* New York: HarperCollins, 1992. Ages 11-14. Slavery, 1807.

Blos, Joan. *A Gathering of Days: A New England Girl's Journal, 1830-32.* New York: Scribner's, 1979. Ages 7-11. U.S. frontier, 1830s.

Collier, James Lincoln, and Christopher Collier. *The Clock.* New York: Delacorte, 1992. Ages 9-12. Connecticut mill life, early 1800s.

De Felice, Cynthia. *Weasel.* New York: Macmillan, 1990. Ages 9-12. Ohio frontier, 1830s.

Fleischman, Paul. *The Borning Room.* New York: Harper, 1991. Ages 11-YA. Ohio, farm life, 1800s.

—. *Coming-and-Going Men: Four Tales.* Illustrated by Randy Gaul. New York: Harper, 1985. Ages 11-YA. Vermont, 1800.

Highwater, Jamake. *Legend Days.* New York: Harper, 1984. Ages 10-YA. U.S., Northern Plains Indians, 1800s.

Hudson, Jan. *Sweetgrass.* New York: Tree Frog Press, 1984; New York: Philomel, 1989. Ages 11-YA. Canada, Dakota Indians, 1830s.

Lyons, Mary E. *Letters from a Slave Girl: The Story of Harriet Jacobs.* New York: Scribner, 1992. Ages 10-13. Slavery in North Carolina, early 1800s.

Moeri, Louise. *Save Queen of Sheba.* New York: Dutton, 1981. Ages 9-12. U.S. frontier, 1800s.

Rinaldi, Ann. *A Stitch in Time.* New York: Scholastic, 1994. Ages 11-14. Family saga set in Salem, Massachusetts, 1788-91.

Van Leeuwen, Jean. *Going West.* Illustrated by Thomas B. Allen. New York: Doubleday/ Dial, 1992. Ages 5-8. Wagon train.

Slavery/Civil War and Post-Civil War/Immigration/ Western Territories (1830s-1914)

Angell, Judie. *One-Way to Ansonia.* New York: Bradbury, 1985. Ages 10-YA. U.S., immigrants, 1890s.

Armstrong, William H. *Sounder.* New York: Harper, 1969. Ages 9-12. U.S. South, African-Americans, early 1900s.

Avi. *The Barn.* New York: Orchard/Richard Jackson, 1994. Ages 9-12. African Americans in the South, early 1900s.

Beatty, Patricia. *Be Ever Hopeful, Hannalee.* New York: Morrow, 1988. Ages 13-YA. Atlanta, Georgia, Post-Civil War era.

-----. *Charley Skedaddle.* New York: Morrow, 1987. Ages 11-14. U.S. Civil War, 1860s.

-----. *Jayhawker.* New York: Morrow, 1991. Ages 10-14. Kansas, slavery, underground railroad, 1800s.

-----. *Turn Homeward, Hannalee.* New York: Morrow, 1984. Ages 10-14. U.S. Civil War, 1860s.

-----. *Who Comes with Cannons?* New York: Morrow, 1992. Ages 9-12. Underground railroad in North Carolina, mid-1800s.

Brenner, Barbara. *Wagon Wheels.* New York: Harper, 1978. Ages 7-9. U.S. pioneers, African Americans, 1870s.

Conlon-McKenna, Marita. *Wildflower Girl.* Illustrated by Donald Teskey. New York: Holiday, 1992. Irish immigrants, mid-19th century.

Conrad, Pam. *Prairie Songs.* New York: Harper, 1985. Ages 10-14. Nebraska frontier life, late 1800s.

-----. *Stonewords: A Ghost Story.* New York: Harper, 1990. Ages 10-YA. Time shift fantasy, 1870s.

De Felice, Cynthia. *Weasel.* New York: Macmillan, 1990. Ages 9-12. Ohio frontier, 1830s.

DeVries, David. *Home at Last.* New York: Dell, 1992. Ages 10-13. Orphan Train, 1800s.

Fleischman, Paul. *Bull Run.* New York: HarperCollins, 1993. Ages 10-14. Civil War era, 1860s.

Fleischman, Sid. *Humbug Mountain.* Boston: Little, 1978. Ages 9-12. Western expansion, St. Louis to Dakota Territory, about 1900.

-----. *Mr. Mysterious & Company.* Boston: Little, 1962. Ages 9-12. Western expansion to California, 1880s.

Forman, James D. *Becca's Story.* New York: Scribner's, 1992. Ages 10-14. Michigan, Civil War era.

Fox, Paula. *The Slave Dancer.* New York: Bradbury, 1973. Ages 11-YA. U.S., slave trade, 1840s.

Fritz, Jean. *Brady.* New York: Coward, 1960. Ages 9-12. Pennsylvania, slavery, 1830s.

Hamilton, Virginia. *The Bells of Christmas.* Illustrated by Lambert Davis. San Diego: Harcourt, 1989. Ages 8-11. Ohio, African Americans, 1890s.

Hansen, Joyce. *The Captive.* New York: Scholastic, 1994. Ages 11-14. Civil War era, slavery.

-----. *Which Way Freedom?* New York: Walker, 1986. Ages 11-YA. U.S., slavery, Civil War era.

Harris, Christie. *Cariboo Trail.* New York: Longman, 1957. Ages 12-14. U.S., Minnesota, western Canada, 1860s.

Harvey, Brett. *Cassie's Journey: Going West in the 1860's.* Illustrated by Deborah Kogan

Ray. New York: Holiday, 1988. Ages 7-9. U.S. frontier, 1860s.

———. *My Prairie Year: Based on the Diary of Elenore Plaisted*. Illustrated by Deborah Kogan Ray. New York: Holiday, 1986. Ages 8-11. Maine to the Dakota Territory, 1889.

Hickman, Janet. *Zoar Blue*. New York: Macmillan, 1978. Ages 9-12. U.S. Civil War era, 1860s.

Holland, Isabelle. *Behind the Lines*. New York: Scholastic, 1994. Ages 11-14. Civil War.

Hunt, Irene. *Across Five Aprils*. Chicago, IL: Follett, 1964. Ages 10-YA. U.S. Civil War era, 1860s.

Hurmence, Belinda. *A Girl Called Boy*. New York: Clarion, 1982. Ages 9-12. Travel back in time to 1850s, slavery, North Carolina.

Irwin, Hadley. *Jim-Dandy*. New York: Macmillan, 1994. Ages 11-14. General Custer, horse story, 1870s.

Kudlinsky, Kathleen V. *Night Bird: A Story of the Seminole Indians*. New York: Viking, 1993. Ages 8-11. Florida's Seminole Indians, 1850s.

Lasky, Kathryn. *Beyond the Divide*. New York: Macmillan, 1983. Ages 10-14. U.S. frontier, mid-1800s.

———. *The Night Journey*. New York: Warne, 1981. Ages 10-14. Russia, United States, early 1900s.

Lawlor, Laurie. *George on His Own*. Niles, IL: Whitman, 1993. Ages 9-12. Homesteading in South Dakota, early 1900s.

Lunn, Janet. *The Root Cellar*. New York: Scribner's, 1983. Ages 10-YA. U.S. Civil War era, 1860s.

MacLachlan, Patricia. *Sarah, Plain and Tall*. New York: Harper, 1985. Ages 7-10. U.S. frontier, 1850s.

———. *Skylark*. New York: HarperCollins, 1994. Ages 8-11. Western frontier, 1850s.

Marzollo, Jean. *Halfway Down Paddy Lane*. New York: Dial, 1981. Ages 12-YA. Travel back in time to New England mill town, 1850.

Monjo, F. N. *The Drinking Gourd*. New York: Harper, 1970. Ages 6-9. New England, underground railroad, 1850s.

Morrow, Honoré. *On to Oregon!* New York: Morrow, 1954. Ages 9-12. U.S. frontier, 1840s.

Myers, Walter Dean. *The Glory Field*. New York: Scholastic, 1994. Ages 11-YA. Civil War era to present.

Nixon, Joan Lowery. *A Family Apart*. New York: Bantam, 1987. Ages 10-13. New York City, Orphan Train, 1860s.

———. *Land of Hope*. New York: Bantam, 1992. Ages 9-12. Russian-Jewish immigrants, early 1900s.

O'Dell, Scott. *Island of the Blue Dolphins*. New York: Houghton, 1960. Ages 10-14. Pacific island, Native Americans, mid-1800s.

O'Dell, Scott. *Sing Down the Moon*. New York: Houghton, 1970. U.S., Navajo Indians, 1860s.

———, and Elizabeth Hall. *Thunder Rolling in the Mountains*. New York: Houghton, 1992. Ages 10-14. Native American movement to reservations, 1870s.

Paterson, Katherine. *Lyddie*. New York: Dutton, 1991. Ages 12-YA. Massachusetts, mill life, mid-1800s.

Paulsen, Gary. *Nightjohn*. New York: Delacorte, 1993. Ages 11-14. Slavery.

Reeder, Carolyn. *Shades of Gray*. New York: Macmillan, 1989. Ages 9-12. U.S. post-Civil War era, 1860s.

Rinaldi, Ann. *In My Father's House*. New York: Scholastic, 1993. Ages 11-14. Civil War Era, 1860s.

Savage, Deborah. *To Race a Dream*. New York: Houghton, 1994. Horse story set in a small Minnesota town, early 1900s.

Sebestyen, Ouida. *Words by Heart*. Boston: Little, 1979. Ages 11-YA. Southwest U.S., African Americans, 1910.

Skurzynski, Gloria. *The Tempering*. New York: Clarion, 1983. Ages 11-YA. Pennsylvania steel mill, 1912.

Smucker, Barbara. *Underground to Canada*. Toronto: Clarke Irwin, 1977. Ages 12-YA.

Canada, Ontario, slavery, 1800s.

Stolz, Mary. *Cezanne Pinto: A Memoir.* New York: Knopf, 1994. Ages 11-14. Georgia plantation, underground railroad, 1860s.

Turner, Ann. *Grasshopper Summer.* New York: Macmillan, 1989. Ages 9-12. U.S., Kentucky to Dakota Territory, 1870s.

Weitzman, David. *Thrashin' Time: Harvest Days in the Dakotas.* Boston: Godine, 1991. Ages 10-13. Western settlements, 1912.

Wilder, Laura Ingalls. *Little House in the Big Woods.* New York: Harper, 1932. Ages 7-10. Wisconsin frontier, 1800s.

Yee, Paul. *Tales from Gold Mountain: Stories of the Chinese in the New World.* Illustrated by Simon Ng. New York: Macmillan, 1990. Chinese on the western frontier, 1800s.

Yep, Lawrence. *Dragonsgate.* New York: HarperCollins, 1993. Ages 9-12. Sierra Nevada mountains, transcontinental railroad, 1867.

-----. *Dragonwings.* New York: Harper, 1979. Ages 9-12. California, early 1900s.

World War I/Prohibition/Great Depression (1914-1939)

Avi. *Shadrach's Crossing.* New York: Pantheon, 1983. Ages 10-YA. U.S. Prohibition and Depression eras, 1932.

Beatty, Patricia. *Eight Mules from Monterey.* New York: Morrow, 1982. Ages 10-YA. U.S., California settlements, 1916.

Frank, Rudolf. *No Hero for the Kaiser.* Translated by Patricia Crampton. Illustrated by Klaus Steffens. New York: Lothrop, 1986 (originally published in 1931). Ages 10-YA. Poland, World War I.

Hesse, Karen. *Letters from Rifka.* New York: Holt, 1992. Ages 9-12. Jewish family fleeing Russia to America, 1919.

Hooks, William H. *Circle of Fire.* New York: Atheneum, 1982. Ages 9-12. Rural North Carolina, Ku Klux Klan, 1930s.

Kerr, Judith. *When Hitler Stole Pink Rabbit.* New York: Coward, 1971. Ages 9-YA. Escape from Germany, 1930s.

Koller, Jackie. *Nothin to Fear.* San Diego: Harcourt, 1991. Ages 10-13. Irish immigrant family in New York City, 1929.

Little, Jean. *From Anna.* New York: Harper, 1972. Ages 9-12. Germany, Canada, 1930s.

Lyon, George Ella. *Borrowed Children.* New York: Watts, 1988. Ages 10-14. Kentucky, Depression era, 1930s.

Myers, Anna. *Red-Dirt Jesse.* New York: Walker, 1993. Ages 9-12. Great Depression in Oklahoma, early 1900s.

Orgel, Doris. *The Devil in Vienna.* New York: Dial, 1978. Ages 11-YA. Pre-World War II Austria/Nazi youth indoctrination, 1938.

Pendergraft, Patricia. *As Far as Mill Springs.* New York: Philomel, 1991. Ages 9-13. East Coast, 1929 depression.

Sebestyen, Ouida. *Far from Home.* Boston: Little, 1980. Ages 12-YA. Texas, Depression era, 1929.

Skurzynski, Gloria. *Good-bye, Billy Radish.* New York: Bradbury, 1992. Ages 9-12. Pennsylvania steel town, World War I.

Snyder, Zilpha Keatly. *Cat Running.* New York: Delacorte, 1994. Ages 9-12. Depression, California, 1933.

Taylor, Mildred. *Song of the Trees.* New York: Dial, 1975. Ages 8-11. Sequels include *Roll of Thunder, Hear My Cry.* Dial, 1976. Ages 9-14; and *Let the Circle Be Unbroken.* Dial, 1981. Ages 10-14. U.S. South, African-Americans, 1930s.

Uchida, Yoshiko. *A Jar of Dreams.* New York: Atheneum, 1981. Ages 10-YA. Sequels include *The Best Bad Thing,* Atheneum, 1983 and *The Happiest Ending,* Atheneum, 1985. San Francisco, Japanese Americans, 1935-1936.

World War II/ Post-World War II/Civil Rights Era/ Vietnam War (1939-1960s)

Avi. *Who Was that Masked Man, Anyway?* New York: Orchard, 1992. Ages 9-12. World War II.

Bauer, Marion Dane. *Rain of Fire.* New York: Clarion, 1983. Ages 10-13. U.S., post-World

War II era.

Bawden, Nina. *Henry.* Illustrated by Joyce Powzyk. New York: Lothrop, 1988. Ages 9-12. England, World War II era.

Bunting, Eve. *The Wall.* Illustrated by Ronald Himler. New York: Clarion, 1990. Ages 7-11. Picture book–a boy and his father visit the Vietnam Veterans Memorial in remembrance.

Coerr, Eleanor. *Meiko and the Fifth Treasure.* New York: Putnam, 1993. Ages 9-12. Nagasaki bombing, World War II.

Davis, Ossie. *Just Like Martin.* New York: Simon & Shuster, 1992. Ages 9-12. Washington, D. C., 1963, Civil Rights.

Frank, Anne. *Anne Frank: The Diary of a Young Girl.* New York: Doubleday, 1952. Ages 10-YA. Germany, World War II.

Garrigue, Sheila. *The Eternal Spring of Mr. Ito.* New York: Bradbury, 1985. Ages 8-11. Canada, Japanese-Canadian internment, World War II.

Gehrts, Barbara. *Don't Say a Word.* Translated by Elizabeth D. Crawford. New York: McElderry, 1975. Ages 13-YA. Germany, World War II.

Greene, Bette. *Summer of My German Soldier.* New York: Dial, 1973. U.S., World War II.

Hahn, Mary Downing. *Stepping on the Cracks.* New York: Clarion, 1991. Ages 10-13. U.S., Maryland, World War II.

Härtling, Peter. *Crutches.* Translated from the German by Elizabeth D. Crawford. New York: Lothrop, 1988. Ages 9-14. Austria, post-World War II.

Hautzig, Esther. *The Endless Steppe.* New York: Harper, 1968. Ages 10-14. Russia, Jews, World War II.

Heuck, Sigrid. *The Hideout.* Translated from the German by Rika Lesser. New York: Dutton, 1988. Ages 9-12. Germany, Jews, World War II.

Houston, Gloria. *But No Candy.* Illustrated by Lloyd Bloom. New York: Philomel, 1992. Ages 6-9. U. S., World War II.

Krisher, Trudy. *Spite Fences.* New York: Delacorte, 1994. Ages 13-YA. Georgia race relations, 1960s.

Levitin, Sonia. *Anne's Promise.* New York: Atheneum, 1993. Ages 10-14. German immigration to U.S., World War II era.

-----. *Journey to America.* New York: Atheneum, 1970. Ages 10-14. Germany, Jews, World War II era.

Lord, Betty Bao. *In the Year of the Boar and Jackie Robinson.* New York: Harper, 1984. Ages 9-12. New York City, Chinese Americans, 1947.

Lowry, Lois. *Number the Stars.* New York: Houghton, 1989. Ages 8-12. Denmark, World War II.

Magorian, Michelle. *Good Night, Mr. Tom.* New York: Harper, 1982. Ages 11-14. England, World War II.

Marko, Katharine McGlade. *Hang out the Flag.* New York: Macmillan, 1992. Ages 9-11. United States, World War II.

Matas, Carol. *Lisa's War.* New York: Scribner's, 1989. Ages 10-13. Denmark, Jews, World War II.

Morpurgo, Michael. *Waiting for Anya.* New York: Viking, 1991. Ages 10-14. Southern France, Jews, World War II.

Myers, Walter Dean. *Fallen Angels.* New York: Scholastic, 1988. Ages 13-YA. Vietnam War era.

Nelson, Vaunda Micheaux. *Mayfield Crossing.* Illustrated by Leonard Jenkins. New York: Putnam, 1993. Ages 9-12. Baseball, school integration, race relations, 1960s.

Orlev, Uri. *The Island on Bird Street.* Translated from the Hebrew by Hillel Halkin. New York: Houghton, 1983. Ages 9-13. Poland, Jews, World War II.

-----. *The Man from the Other Side.* Translated from the Hebrew by Hillel Halkin. New York: Houghton, 1991. Ages 12-YA. Poland, Jews, World War II.

Paulsen, Gary. *The Cookcamp.* New York: Orchard, 1991. Ages 10-13. U.S., road crew, World War II.

Pelgrom, Els. *The Winter When Time Was Frozen.* Translated from the Dutch by Maryka and Rafael Rudnik. New York: Morrow, 1980. Ages 9-12. Holland, World War II.

Perera, Hilda. *Kiki: A Cuban Boy's Adventures in America*. Translated from the Spanish by Warren Hampton and Hilda Gonzales. Illustrated by Mathieu Nuygen. New York: Pickering, 1992. Miami, Cuba, and Florida's Seminole and Miccosukee tribes, 1960s.

Reiss, Johanna. *The Upstairs Room*. New York: Crowell, 1972. Ages 10-14. Holland, Jews, World War II.

Reuter, Bjarne. *The Boys from St. Petri*. Translated from the Danish by Anthea Bell. New York: Dutton, 1994. Ages 12-YA. Denmark, World War II era.

Richter, Hans Peter. *Friedrich*. Translated from the German by Edite Kroll. New York: Holt, 1970. Ages 10-14. Germany, Jews, World War II.

—————. *I Was There*. Translated by Edite Kroll. New York: Holt, 1972. Ages 10-14. Germany, World War II.

Ross, Ramon Royal. *Harper & Moon*. New York: Atheneum, 1993. Ages 10-YA. World War II.

Salisbury, Graham. *Under the Blood-Red Sun*. New York: Delacorte, 1994. Japanese residents of Hawaii, World War II era.

Siegal, Aranka. *Upon the Head of the Goat: A Childhood in Hungary 1939-1944*. New York: Farrar, 1981. Ages 10-14. Hungary, World War II.

Slepian, Jan. *Risk n' Roses*. New York: Putnam, 1990. Ages 11-14. Bronx, New York, 1948.

Talbert, Marc. *The Purple Heart*. New York: HarperCollins, 1992. Ages 10-13. U.S., Vietnam War era.

Uchida, Yoshiko. *Journey to Topaz*. Illustrated by Donald Carrick. New York: Scribner's, 1971. Ages 10-14. U.S., internment of Japanese Americans, World War II.

Vos, Ida. *Anna Is Still There*. Translated from the Dutch by Terese Idelstein and Inez Smidt. New York: Houghton, 1993. Ages 10-13. Holland, Post- World War II.

—————. *Hide and Seek*. Translated from the Dutch by Terese Edelstein and Inez Smidt. New York: Houghton, 1991. Ages 9-13. Jews, World War II.

Wiesel, Elie. *Night*. New York: Bantam, 1982/ 1960. Ages 12-YA. Hungary, German concentration camps, World War II.

Yolen, Jane. *The Devil's Arithmetic*. New York: Viking, 1988. Ages 12-YA. Time shift to Poland, concentration camps, World War II.

Young, Ronder Tomas. *Learning by Heart*. New York: Houghton, 1993. Ages 9-12. South, 1960s.

Sources for Narrative Literature Related to World History

In the following children's literature textbooks, the end-of-chapter lists, annotated for historical settings, recommend many titles of historical fiction works based on world history.

Cullinan, Beatrice. *Literature and the Child*. 2nd ed. Harcourt Brace Jovanovich, 1989. Chapter 9–Historical Fiction and Biography.

Lynch-Brown, Carol and Carl M. Tomlinson. *Essentials of Children's Literature*. Allyn and Bacon, 1993. Chapter 8–Historical Fiction.

Norton, Donna E. *Through the Eyes of a Child: An Introduction to Children's Literature*. Macmillan, 1991. Chapter 10–Historical Fiction.

Sutherland, Zena and May Hill Arbuthnot. *Children and Books*. 7th ed. Scott Foresman, 1986. Chapter 12–Historical Fiction.

For award-winning works and authors (both U.S. and international), *Reference Guide to Historical Fiction for Children and Young Adults* by Lynda G. Adamson (New York: Greenwood, 1987) provides lengthy reviews, including the historical facts treated in each book. Another useful reference work is *World History for Children and Young Adults* by Vandelia VanMeter (Littleton, CO: Libraries Unlimited, 1991).

An excellent source for recently published historical narratives is the annual list of "Notable Children's Trade Books in the Field of

Social Studies" developed by a committee of the National Council for the Social Studies. This list presents brief reviews of useful and worthy books related to the social studies and published in the preceding year. The list can be found in the April/May issue of *Social Education* and is arranged by topics, such as World History, Culture, and Life, Anthropology, and North American Culture, History, and Life.

Nonfiction trade books often provide other historical narratives, such as biographies. Beverly Kobrin's *Eyeopeners! How to Choose and Use Children's Books About Real People* (New York: Penguin, 1988) briefly annotates and arranges by categories more than 500 nonfiction titles. Although these titles are related to many content areas, they are nicely categorized for easy retrieval.

References

Atwell, Nancie. *In the Middle: Writing, Reading, and Learning with Adolescents.* Portsmouth, NH: Boynton/Cook, 1987.

Britton, James N. *Language and Learning.* London: Allen Lane, 1980.

Brozo, William G., and Carl M. Tomlinson. "Literature: The Key to Lively Content Courses." *The Reading Teacher* 40(December 1986): 288-293.

Bruner, Jerome. *Actual Minds, Possible Worlds.* Cambridge, MA: Harvard University Press, 1986.

Cianciolo, Patricia. "Yesterday Comes Alive for Readers of Historical Fiction." *Language Arts* 58(April 1981): 452-461.

Downs, Anita. "Breathing Life into the Past: The Creation of History Units Using Trade Books." Chapter in *The Story of Ourselves: Teaching History Through Children's Literature,* edited by Michael O. Tunnell and Richard Ammon. Portsmouth, NH: Heinemann, 1993.

Freeman, Evelyn B., and Linda Levstik. "Recreating the Past: Historical Fiction in the Social Studies Curriculum." *The Elementary School Journal* 88(March 1988): 329-337.

Huck, Charlotte S., Susan Hepler, and Janet Hickman. *Children's Literature in the Elementary School.* 5th ed. Orlando, FL: Harcourt Brace Jovanovich, 1993.

Levstik, Linda S. "The Relationship Between Historical Response and Narrative in a Sixth Grade Classroom." *Theory and Research in Social Education* 41(September 1986): 1-15.

Levstik, Linda S. "A Child's Approach to History." *The Social Studies* 74(May/June 1983): 232-236.

Lynch-Brown, Carol. "Using Literature Across the Curriculum." Chapter in *Reading and the Middle School Student: Strategies to Enhance Literacy* by Judith L. Irvin. Boston: Allyn and Bacon, 1990.

Lynch-Brown, Carol, and Carl M. Tomlinson. *Essentials of Children's Literature.* Needham Heights, MA: Allyn and Bacon, 1993.

Moffett, James. *Teaching the Universe of Discourse.* Boston: Houghton Mifflin, 1968.

National Council for the Social Studies. "Social Studies for Early Childhood and Elementary School Children Preparing for the 21st Century." *Social Education* 53, (January 1989): 14-23.

Pappas, Christine C., Barbara Z. Kiefer, and Linda S. Levstik. "More Ideas to Integrate Curricular Areas." Chapter in *An Integrated Language Perspective in the Elementary School: Theory into Action.* New York: Longman, 1990.

Ravitch, Diane, and Chester E. Finn, Jr. *What Do Our 17-Year-Olds Know?* New York: Harper & Row, 1987.

Tomlinson, Carl M., Michael O. Tunnell, and Donald J. Richgels. "The Content and Writing of History in Textbooks and Trade Books." Chapter in *The Story of Ourselves: Teaching History Through Children's Literature,* edited by Michael O. Tunnell and Richard Ammon. Portsmouth, NH: Heinemann, 1993.

◼ Contributors

Judith L. Irvin teaches courses in Curriculum, Leadership, and Middle Level Education at Florida State University. She is the author of *Reading and the Middle School Student* and *Transforming Middle Level Education* (Allyn and Bacon) as well as numerous articles on content area reading instruction.

John P. Lunstrum teaches courses in Reading and Social Studies Education at Florida State University. He co-authored *Teaching Reading in the Social Studies* (1978), published by the International Reading Association and ERIC Clearinghouse, as well as numerous articles on critical language processes and the use of controversy in the social studies.

Carol Lynch-Brown teaches courses in Children's Literature at Florida State University. She is the co-author of *Essentials of Children's Literature* (Allyn and Bacon) as well as numerous articles on the use of Children's Literature to support the teaching of content areas. She is the Southeastern Coordinator of the Teachers' Choices Project (International Reading Association).

Mary Friend Shepard teaches courses at Thomas College (Georgia) in Elementary Social Studies with special emphasis on the integration of art and music into social studies themes. She also teaches elementary teachers how to make mainstreaming and inclusion of special needs children successful in elementary classrooms.